SO BOLD AN AIM

HEADQUARTERS OF THE FOOD AND AGRICULTURE ORGANIZATION OF THE UNITED NATIONS, ROME

SO BOLD AN AIM

*Ten Years of International Co-operation
Toward Freedom from Want*

FOOD AND AGRICULTURE ORGANIZATION
OF THE UNITED NATIONS

Quebec 1945   Rome 1955

© FAO 1955

Printed in Italy
STABILIMENTO TIPOGRAFICO FAUSTO FAILLI — ROMA

CONTENTS

INTRODUCTION		1
AUTHOR'S NOTE		3
Chapter I	TWO REVOLUTIONS	5
II	MAN ORGANIZES HIMSELF	12
III	A FUSION OF IDEAS	25
IV	FORMATIVE INFLUENCES: SHORTAGES, POPULATION GROWTH AND UNDER-DEVELOPED COUNTRIES	53
V	SHORTAGES AND SURPLUSES	75
VI	INTELLIGENCE SERVICE	92
VII	TECHNICAL ACTIVITIES	107
VIII	SPRINGBOARD FOR ACTION	138
IX	THE MARCH OF EVENTS	153

Appendices:

I	List of Member Nations	163
II	Selected List of Publications	164
III	Training Centres	171

" There have been functional international agencies with more circumscribed objectives and tasks, but FAO is the first which sets out with so bold an aim as that of helping nations to achieve freedom from want. Never before have the nations got together for such a purpose. "

Lester B. Pearson of Canada,
Chairman, First Session
of the Conference

INTRODUCTION

In requesting Mr. P. Lamartine Yates to prepare this "Tenth Anniversary" book on the influences which contributed to the creation of The Food and Agriculture Organization of the United Nations (FAO) and conditioned its activities during its first decade I was anxious to secure the services of someone who possessed an intimate knowledge of the Organization and yet could appraise its developments, achievements and shortcomings from a somewhat detached point of view. Mr. Yates was a member of the staff of FAO from its formation — first in the Economics Division and later in the Director-General's Office. He resigned in 1951 when the Headquarters of the Organization was transferred to Rome and has since been employed by the United Kingdom Colonial Development Corporation where his work has given him an insight, from a different point of view, into many of the problems with which FAO is today concerned. No present member of the staff could have combined the two requirements I had in mind, quite apart from being able, in the present pressure of work, to devote the necessary time to such an undertaking. I therefore count myself fortunate in having been able to obtain Mr. Yates' services.

At the same time any individual writer's interpretation of influences and trends must be coloured by his own experience, environment and outlook. No two individuals would be likely to view through identical spectacles the varied and varying panorama of the last and the coming decades. This is not a volume of cold facts, of historical data, or of persons and places. The factual story of FAO's progress has been told elsewhere and will no doubt be related again in more detail in the coming years.

What this book attempts to do is not to recount FAO's brief history, but to assess its significance in relation to the endeavours of men and nations in striving for higher standards of living. In issuing this book as an official FAO publication I recognize that it is necessarily a personal interpretation and one from which others may dissent in smaller or larger degree. But still others, I believe, will accept it in general terms as an illuminating account of some very important happenings.

It is with these thoughts in mind that I commend this volume to the member countries of FAO and the wider public which is interested in our Organization. In doing so I believe that it will provide not merely a backward and forward look on the occasion of our Tenth Anniversary, but a thought-provoking stimulus for all who have at heart the ideals which created and have fostered the effort we are making to provide humanity with those essential elements for achieving the good life — more and better food, homes and clothing.

P. V. Cardon
Director-General

AUTHOR'S NOTE

This book sets out to describe the ideas and events which caused FAO to come into existence and those which since its birth have moulded the activities of the Organization into their present shape. The book does not attempt to portray the work currently being done in all the subject fields; that would require a much longer volume. Thus the reader will not find here any account of the several and collective activities of Member Governments nor of the particular programmes of the technical divisions in the Secretariat. These are described in special Conference documents and elsewhere.

I wish to take this opportunity of expressing my most sincere thanks to the Director-General, Deputy Director-General, division directors and their staff for the trouble they have taken to make information available and for their wise advice on many aspects of the text.

P. LAMARTINE YATES

Chapter I

TWO REVOLUTIONS

Man is a striving animal. He strives to better his condition, to outdo his neighbours, to vanquish his enemies, to master nature, to understand the why and wherefore of material phenomena. He strives also to attain a higher spiritual state, to do good to others, to overcome selfishness, to secure fairer shares to all and justice in the settlement of disputes. These two motives, material advancement and moral improvement, provide the mainspring in a large sector of human activity.

The FAO activity represents one modest instance of this striving: comparatively modest because, although significant indeed in the international scene of the last ten years, it is very young in the time-scale of history. It is an instance which combines, as will be seen, these two motives of man's endeavour, the material and the spiritual; the urge to obtain more worldly goods — in this case food and the other products of soil and water — with the urge to help other peoples, particularly those less advantaged. And FAO had to be created as a vehicle for this striving because the radically changed condition of the world makes old vehicles as obsolete as the stage-coach. New times, new institutions.

Not that man has striven unremittingly for material and spiritual betterment. There have been long periods in history when for no obvious reason the urge has weakened and he has stagnated. Some hold that progress and pause alternate in cycles with the rise and fall of civilizations.

China, Babylon, Egypt, the Andes, Europe, have each in their time experienced great forward surges in knowledge, wealth and culture while between the crests of these waves the impetus has been lost, the vision faded. Some groups of human beings have been more imbued with these urges than others; and it is not easily explained why some have acquired mastery over nature and have accumulated wealth while others have not. The African peoples have hitherto shared less in the movement; except for the northern shore it has not been a continent through which run highways of major migration.

But during the last 200 years, roughly since 1750, man's striving has acquired a new setting and a new tempo. There have been two explosive revolutions, one in the sciences and another in thought.

As to the scientific revolution, man has forged tools out of his technical discoveries which have allowed him immensely to increase his control over nature and to produce goods as never before. The locus of this explosion was Europe whence it has spread outward, carried by European peoples to the places where they settled and passed by them to other peoples, till now not a land, not a tribe, but has experienced the contact.

The story of the scientific revolution has been told often enough. Its progress has been geometric and still is, whether measured by output of goods, harnessing of power (coal, electricity, oil), medical protection and — a result of these — the expansion of population which previously had been static for centuries. World population has been estimated at 694 million in 1750, 1,094 million in 1850 and 2,454 million in 1950.[1] Geographically, this outburst has accompanied economic and medical developments; the brakes came off first in Europe and then in country after country, till today there are few where the rate of population increase does not exceed one percent per annum.

Yet, in spite of this multiplication of heads, there are more goods per head, far more, than when it all began in the eighteenth century. This statement, however, requires qualification. By no means all countries have experienced growth in real income per head. It has occurred chiefly in Europe and the territories of European settlement, plus Japan. Until very recently the other parts of the world continued to live, or rather to exist, in the same poverty as for centuries. And, when the new knowledge came to them, it was the medicine man, controlling death, who made the first and larger impact before the industrialist set up his turbine.

The second explosive revolution, that in the realm of thought, stems from the European philosophers of the eighteenth century, perhaps from Jean-Jacques Rousseau more than anyone else, who gave a new interpretation to Christian ethics. Two features of the new teaching were to have special significance: first, that all men are

---

[1] *World Population Conference* (Rome, September 1954). Doc. E/Conf. 13/243.

in an important sense equal, which doctrine soon acquired the addendum that they should have equal opportunity; second, that "doing good" should not be a characteristic solely of individual behaviour in respect of personal conduct and charity toward others, but should become a recognized function of public institutions, in fact that the State had responsibilities for the well-being (not merely the protection) of its citizens. Taken together, the two doctrines have intertwined to produce on the one hand, social legislation with its attendant institutions, and, on the other, the great economic endeavour of our time: the attempt to help the under-developed countries achieve the opportunities and create the material goods hitherto enjoyed only by developed countries.

It were idle to pretend that the sense of community among nations is very strongly developed yet; men are not ready to vote for international redistribution of income on the massive scale they tolerate, nay often welcome, within the nation-state. It would be surprising if they did, since they have been doing it for only a short time, comparatively speaking, in their own communities. The fact that the United States economic aid programme and the bilateral aid programmes of other nations have already been launched is itself remarkable enough. Likewise, the technical assistance activities of the United Nations and what are called the "specialized agencies" set up by governments can be regarded in large part as manifestations of the same moral urge, the urge to carry help beyond fellow-nationals to the farthest corners of the earth.

This moral feeling has focused on an objective having strong emotional content, arousing the missionary fervour of scientists and social workers alike. For the raising of the living standards of the less advantaged sector of the world is, and will remain for the rest of this century and longer, a central issue in world affairs. It is their turn now. The under-developed countries have become politically vocal; many have recently gained political independence. Together they command an overwhelming majority of votes in any world assembly of nations. Their striving for self-advancement has become a No. 1 national and international issue and they will see to it that it remains so.

Not that international aid alone can activate their economic development; it cannot even be the principal factor. It can prime the pump; it can be the gunpowder train, but in the end each nation has to provide from within its own resources the vast bulk of the capital and skills and manpower required. An "operation bootstrap."

Science is now beginning to be applied to the problems of the under-developed countries, as it began in northwest Europe 200 years ago. The revolution has reached them. Their peoples now crave material progress, cash incomes and the paraphernalia of twentieth century "civilization." Thus one of the revolutions is stirring the under-developed peoples to new forms of activity while the other revolution impels the advanced countries to extend aid.

Many are pessimistic as to the capacity of the under-developed countries to climb out of primary poverty and, capacity apart, as to the possibility of their doing so. They point to the apparently meagre mineral resources of many of those countries, the eroded lands and unfriendly climates, the rapidly expanding population on territory in many cases already overcrowded, the absence and impossibility of saving on a scale to provide the capital required, the hopelessness of finding enough exports to pay for needed imports of equipment for industry, and many more equally convincing arguments. It is no good seeking a head-on refutation of these arguments. It may, however, be pertinent to enquire what the outlook was in Europe 200 years ago when she started pulling herself up by her bootstraps. Could it not be said then that her peoples were too poor to save on any massive scale, that her agriculture could not be made more fruitful and her peoples would not adapt to factory tasks and urban ways of life? And yet the revolution took place.

Is the plight of the under-developed countries today any worse than that of Europe in 1750?

True there are no vast prairie lands in temperate zones waiting to be ploughed, nor are there empty spaces into which to move surplus population on a massive scale. But Europe had gone far down the road to industrialization before she had much recourse to importing food and exporting people. Today agriculture has other tools for increasing production without having to rely on new acres by the million. Also the newer forms of power for industry — oil and still more atomic energy — mean that industry can be located where the people are, not *vice versa*. Moreover, there are nations standing by who have already modernized themselves and who can lend their skills and experience for the job.

All these things give solid ground for believing that during the next 100 years there could happen in the remaing two-thirds of the world what hitherto has happened in only one-third — a revolution in modes of living, in standards of living, social patterns, arts and skills, culture and thought. If this be a fair assessment, it is just about the most exciting prospect for a century-to-be that mankind has ever faced. By comparison, most of our other preoccupations appear puny indeed; cold war, class war, colour prejudice, religious intolerance and so on. What is almost within human grasp is nothing less than the abolition of primary poverty in the last strongholds of poverty, the bringing of the low-income peoples, not to equality of income with the wealthiest peoples, but to within hailing distance, so that there is no longer a wide social and material gap between them.

This is what is at stake. And this was one, if not the principal, motive in establishing the specialized agencies of the United Nations. They are weapons of this increasingly articulated policy, important weapons deployed in vital sectors of the campaign offensive.

Chapter II

MAN ORGANIZES HIMSELF

One school of thought maintains that international institutions generally are a waste of taxpayers' money, providing comfortable sinecures for displaced bureaucrats and extra vacation opportunities for jaded government delegates. In order to fabricate reasons for continuing in existence, it is alleged, these institutions convene conference after conference where nothing is achieved but platitudinous oratory, and issue publications which are never read and would serve no useful purpose if they were.

Another school of thought argues that United Nations agencies and other international bodies must of necessity fail for lack of executive authority; they are a waste because only world government can deal with world problems, a government to which all national legislatures would be subordinate. Nation-states must inevitably merge themselves into the World-State; it is only a matter of time.

Perhaps, fortunately, neither of these doctrines is as true as the middle position, which may be hard to define in precise terms and may have little emotional appeal.

International agencies have come into existence to meet specific requirements of the present age. Men have found that they need these additional administrative instruments in their attempt to regulate and control their environment. Such agencies represent an extension from organizations at the national level where controls proliferate and men submit in so many spheres to a discipline instead of acting uninhibitedly, arrange their affairs instead of leaving them to chance. FAO came into existence to meet one of these present-day needs.

The industrial revolution brought a host of tools and gadgets into men's hands which in turn forced the establishment of new rules and organizations. Thus the multiplication of horse-drawn coaches impelled the establishment of a rule of the road, even if it remains unclear why some peoples gravitated left and others right! The advent of the railway necessitated a time-table, of the motor-car a speed limit and driving tests, of the aircraft a system of traffic lanes and safety regulations. The expansion of businesses beyond what a family or private company could cope with brought the joint-stock company into existence, the public holding of and trading in stocks and shares created stock exchanges and so on. All these new rules and organizations enable man to operate more conveniently the new techniques he has acquired. Scientific research too has become so complex that workers combine in teams to achieve their goals and organize the exchange of information with other groups through the medium of conferences or technical papers.

Another motive has operated powerfully to build up organizations and that is the ethical principle noted in the previous chapter — the desire to obtain fairer shares for various sectors of the community. It was this motive which created producers' and consumers' co-operatives. The same gave rise to the modern state's social services, at first voluntary ones by charitable organizations, later superseded by governmental services in health, education and insurance. It has brought protection to infant industries and subsidies to depressed ones. More recent manifestations of the principle of fair shares are price control, rationing and the queue. Belligerents in World War II submitted to tighter controls than in World War I largely in order to secure fairer shares of scarce supplies and to achieve some measure of equity in distribution of burdens and sacrifices.

While men in their nation-states have been progressively accepting more and more organization in face of the double compulsion of the technological and ethical revolutions, they have more tardily perceived the need for international organization for similar purposes. Obvious needs were recognized first: the International Postal Union, rules for navigation on the oceans, international quarantine regulations, and the many *ad hoc* congresses of the late nineteenth century at which scientists exchanged knowledge and experience on techniques of research with colleagues from other lands.

Gradually, however, traffic between nations in goods and people and ideas has thickened. The world shrinks until its farthest corners become economically interdependent. Copenhagen links with Capetown, Basra with Buenos Aires. Nations get together with their neighbours for specific purposes, for instance, Benelux and the European Coal and Steel Community; they get together in world-wide gatherings at least for discussion if not for rule enforcement. It is only in recent decades that nations have felt the necessity of permanent international agencies with permanent secretariats in economic and social fields. Now we have quite a family of them but haphazard in the ground they cover. Thus labour, food and agriculture, health, weather, aviation and education are taken care of, to name but a few, but much less is done in the great field of industry, or in land communication, or in national finance.

In these agencies can be discerned the same pair of motives as in national organization: organization to acquire more scientific knowledge by international dissemination and thereby to accelerate the adoption of more efficient practices and, secondly, organization for "doing good" in some ethical sense — advanced nations helping less advantaged ones, bringing of economic and other benefits to the "have-nots," fairer shares internationally. What exotic fruit to grow out of the seeds sown by the philosophers of the French and American revolutions!

One may not conclude that there exists in all this an ineluctable tendency toward more and more cordial human co-operation in ever-widening spheres of activity. There is no evidence of straight line progression from family to village, village to town, town to county, county to nation, nation to continental region, region to world. It is more complex than that. The national integration and consequent organization create interests and obligations which in many senses make it harder rather than easier to proceed thence to combine in international agencies and accept their obligations. For example, when governments have adopted import duties and quotas and exchange control as instruments of national policy for full employment and balance of payments equilibrium, it will be hard for them to join an international agency which expects its members immediately or even progressively to renounce such measures in order to further greater freedom of international trade, non-discrimination and the economic independence of weaker countries. Again, governments which, in addition to adopting the above measures, have also incurred obligations to protect their farmers against foreign competition may find it hard to get together with other governments in agreeing upon terms for an international commodity agreement designed to expand rather than restrict trade in that product at fair and stable prices. By the time nations have clothed themselves in full-scale national economic armour, they may be well protected against their enemies but they may find it well-nigh impossible to shake hands with their friends.

Equality of opportunity would also require that labour could freely move into the most advantageous market, but while such freedom has largely been achieved within nations where the last remnants of caste barriers are breaking down, there is less freedom of international movement now than there was 50 years ago. Above all, foreign entry into the great United States labour market has been heavily restricted with powerful effects on the relative level of wages as between that market and others.

Capital, too, which should move unhindered if men are to reap the benefits of equal opportunity, is more fettered and restrained than in any previous peacetime period. At one end we see restrictions on capital exports imposed for balance of payments control purposes and at the other we find many countries imposing highly deterrent conditions on capital imports in the name of national independence.

As Gunnar Myrdal has said : "The process of national integration makes the need for international integration ever greater but, at the same time, increases tremendously the difficulties of accomplishing it." [1]

Nor is this all. The extent to which the new international agencies can be used depends upon the psychological attitudes of member nations. If the desire be weak, the machinery will be little used. It is not many decades ago when even in the most organized countries there was no strong public feeling in favour of "organizing for equality," when such things as trade unions, social insurance, public education services were disapproved of, when poverty was held to be solely the result of personal incapacity and could have nothing to do with the system and its institutions. The change from those attitudes has taken place within the last 100 years, not a long period in the context of history.

In respect of relationships between peoples of different nations the feeling of belonging to one single family is still quite weak. Experience of individuals does not bring them into frequent contact with the outside world. Even in countries depending most on foreign trade the majority

---

[1] *See* G. MYRDAL : *Toward a more closely integrated free-world economy* (prepared for presentation at Conference III, Columbia University Bicentennial, April 1954) in which this whole question is comprehensively discussed.

take for granted the imported goods they use, while foreign affairs are an ineffective subject on which to seek election to parliament. Not many people, statistically speaking, travel abroad; the far-away countries are still far away. Consequently ordinary citizens are only partially ready to appreciate the need for extending the national organizations, with which they are newly preoccupied, into international organizations charged with similar duties at the world level. Either or both of two reactions are natural. Some will say it is waste of public money to give aid to foreign peoples or to contribute to maintenance of international secretariats. Others will deprecate any commitments through international agreements to courses of action which might limit the home government's freedom of action in dealing with national emergencies, for they have from experience grounds for fear that a nation will have trouble enough coping with economic difficulties that might arise, without the added complication of trying to honour previously assumed pledges to other countries.

These two slogans of "small budgets" and "no commitments" constantly recur, naked or disguised, in the statements of governments' delegates at United Nations agency meetings. And though these attitudes may at times exasperate and frustrate those in charge of the agencies' secretariats, it is cause for surprise and for some gratification that they are not heard even more. It is as remarkable as it is fortunate that public opinion supports international action on the present scale. The contrast in attitudes and achievements between the post-World War I decade and the post-World War II decade is striking indeed.

It can be argued that during the latter period the need for concerted international action has been greater and that the achievement, howsoever significant, has not matched the need. But this represents a normal phenomenon of history, namely that events march several steps ahead of man's capacity or willingness to deal with them.

Despite these somewhat conflicting tendencies, it seems reasonable to expect that the desire for international action will strengthen rapidly during the coming decade or two. International intercourse of men, goods, ideas, will become more complicated and will generate — with some timelag — patterns of thought which not merely accept but demand a proliferation of intergovernmental activities to facilitate more commodious life on this planet.

* * *

Now let us turn to consider how all this applies to food and agriculture, first within the nation and then internationally.

Agriculture has felt a need for special assistance and support more than any other branch of economic activity. As soon as farming ceases to be almost the sole occupation of a society, as soon as expanding industries attract away from agriculture labour and capital and skills, farmers find themselves in a weak bargaining position. If nothing were done about it there would be no sort of equilibrium and the farming community would be perpetually disadvantaged.

Man's demands for goods other than food are always increasing faster than his demand for food ; these other sectors of the economy therefore have to expand faster than farming; they have to absorb more labour and capital and in a free economy they do so by offering higher returns to those means of production. Thus, those who remain behind on the land have to accept lower incomes and a lower return on their capital than do their colleagues in industry and trade. Left to its own devices, farming in most countries and at most periods of history — though there are exceptions — would be and has been a depressed industry.

Yet the farmer is needed in an emergency. In time of war he may be called upon suddenly to expand his output, which many nations regard as a powerful reason for shielding him in peacetime from the more violent forces of the market.

There is another reason for farmers needing aid. Both the acquisition and the dissemination of technical knowledge must be reckoned more difficult in agriculture than in industry. As to acquisition by means of laboratory research and field experiment, industry has got itself organized into units large enough and rich enough to sponsor research from its own resources, whereas there are few farmers operating on a scale enabling them to contemplate anything of the kind. Nor is it just a question of cost. There is a much longer time span in agricultural research; one particular experiment often may extend over several years before a result is obtained. For these reasons the State has found itself constrained to organize and finance agricultural research on a much more extensive scale than it has for industry.

As to the dissemination of knowledge, this too is more difficult in agriculture. So much of industry is built in large units which either carry on their own research or have on their staffs men whose job it is to keep informed of technical developments in the relevant field and who have the training to apply them to the needs of their firm. Farms are quite different from firms. Farms are small, even large ones are no size at all compared with large-scale industry; they lack resources for doing experimental work and do not retain staff to follow technical developments. Moreover, farms are geographically scattered; in many a highly concentrated industry one can cover two-thirds of its output by visiting five or six factories; in farming, one would have to make visits running into hundreds of thousands, spread over a great part of the country.

Farms, then, are weak economically and they are also weak technically. Consequently, special efforts have been made to counteract these weaknesses. The organization and financing of agricultural research has from the outset been a function of governments, supplemented of recent years by the useful research programmes of the industries manufacturing farm requisites. Governments, in countries where they can afford it, also have established extension or advisory services, whose staffs bring to farmers the practical application of the findings of the research workers. Expensive though this be, it has been found the most effective way of speeding technical progress among the hundreds of thousands of small-scale producers. In a few countries farmers themselves help in spreading knowledge of improved techniques; for instance, through their co-operative societies or local farmers' clubs which organize meetings and visits.

Then there are the nation-wide farm organizations through which the producers' viewpoints can be articulated on major issues of agricultural policy, for here too farmers have found that through strong organizations they are better able to attract public and governmental attention to their problems. Whatever form they take — bodies representing producers of a single product, unions of hired workers, associations of farmers of a particular political or religious persuasion, or more general all-embracing unions — they have a common characteristic in seeking to obtain for their members economic advantages greater than would be theirs in a free market system of unorganized individuals.

In so doing, generally speaking, they obtain sympathetic hearing from governments who, in all the more advanced countries, have traditionally been prepared to employ public power and public funds to strengthen agriculture against its endemic weaknesses. In the nineteenth century it was the protection of agriculture which provided the first instance of not adhering to, or departing from, the theoretically acceptable doctrines of free trade. Agricultural protection by means of import duties and later quantitative restriction was early built into the economic systems of continental European countries and in due time spread over the world.

But it became apparent that defence against foreign competition was not enough; on the one hand, the agricultural population remained a depressed low-income group to trouble urban consciences; on the other, it was realized that the technical efficiency of a great number of farmers was lamentable and that if public money was to be devoted to agriculture it must stimulate efficiency as well as raise incomes. That is how governments have evolved the comprehensive battery of aid programmes which now in so many countries buttress the agricultural industry — marketing schemes, subsidies, tax reliefs, price-support programmes and the like.

In under-developed countries the process has not yet gone so far partly because the need is not yet so pressing — industries only just beginning — and partly because governments in those countries lack public funds, due to low national incomes, on a scale sufficient for such tasks. However, there seems no reason to suppose that the development of governmental intervention will not follow a similar course in these as in the wealthier countries. Unquestionably agriculture constitutes the most cared-for and protected sector of the economy.

Which does not mean to say that it is over-organized, over-cared for. That might be arguable if we saw incomes in agriculture higher than in other sectors and a rate of technical progress more rapid than in industry. In spite of all the representations, sometimes vociferous, of the farming community and of all the aid programmes devised by governments, agriculture is still in almost all countries the least advantaged sector, the least well furnished with modern techniques and the least well paid.

Of course some forms of aid tend to bring about a situation opposite from that desired; some tend to ossify the existing structure of the industry, or a part of it, and to establish penalties against individual enterprise and technical progress. That is a recognized and constant danger. It is not a reason for denying assistance, though it may suggest the need for more skilful designing and administration of the aid programmes.

Now, just as government programmes for agriculture have evolved over the years in response to a keenly felt need, so also later and more gradually a need has come to be felt for international organization and international programmes. This has taken a multitude of forms which still today are branching out into new types of co-operation between nations; but broadly they can be considered under three heads : first, joint action — the need for intergovernmental programmes of technical control (e.g. against pests and diseases of animals and plants) and of economic control (e.g. commodity agreements and surplus disposal programmes); second, the collection and dissemination of information using a variety of media — international meetings, publications, visits; thirdly, the acquiring of expertise principally by the less developed countries from the more developed.

But the growth of ideas and practice in relation to international organization for agriculture requires a separate chapter to itself.

Chapter III

A FUSION OF IDEAS

In order to understand what FAO was set up to do and what work lies ahead some account must be given of the influences which led to its establishment. However, it is not possible in a sketch of this kind to provide a history of all the international activities in food and agriculture, though no doubt that will one day be done. It must be sufficient here to select and briefly describe some of the more significant landmarks during the present century to illustrate how thought and action have gradually evolved in relation to these matters. Particularly in tracing the development of a group of ideas the act of selection entails the danger that important tributaries of thought will be left out. The confluence of assorted ideas in the creation of an organization always presents a highly complex genetic process in which the passing on and growth of individual elements can be only in part discerned; and in the present case there may well have been important formative ideas which have no memorial. With that warning and apology let us attempt to disentangle what happened.

Already before the opening of this century there had grown up a considerable amount of intercourse among agricultural scientists and technicians from different lands. The first International Veterinary Congress was held in 1863 at Hamburg and initiated an unbroken series of world veterinary congresses. The problems of sugar producers resulted in what is perhaps the earliest intergovernmental commodity agreement on record (signed in 1864).

A common interest in improving farm methods and a conviction that the emerging scientific and technological discoveries could contribute powerfully thereto provided the principal motive at that date for international contact among agricultural groups. Progressive farmers were making energetic efforts to achieve advantages through more efficient production. The findings of biology and biochemistry were increasingly applied. Better breeds of farm animals and better varieties of crops were being introduced. Yields of wheat, which had been static from Nero to Napoleon at around 10 bushels per acre, had risen to 15 bushels by 1850 and averaged 20 to 30 bushels in some European countries by 1900. Today, yields in some countries exceed 50 bushels per acre.

Technical matters contributing to higher farm productivity and greater efficiency of production formed the bulk of discussion at early European-centred international agricultural gatherings. Groups interested in agriculture, horticulture, viticulture, arboriculture, sylviculture, aviculture, sericulture, pisciculture, dairying, the combatting of plant and animal diseases, insect pests, meteorology and plant and animal breeding were among those drawn together internationally prior to 1900. Particular examples of these international congresses are the Hydrographers Congress of 1893 to study marine life in the Baltic and

North Atlantic, the Congress of European Forest Experiment Stations and Research Organizations held in Namur in 1883 and the International Co-operative Alliance founded in London in 1895.

But the first two international organizations to represent the *general* interests of agriculture owed their origin in large part to the severe agricultural depression in the 'eighties and 'nineties. The formation of the International Commission of Agriculture in 1889 stemmed from the efforts of private individuals and groups particularly in Europe, who had become strongly convinced of the need for organization to offset the inherent economic weaknesses of the industry and to deal with the common problems of agriculturalists all over the world. The International Institute of Agriculture (IIA), established in Rome in 1905, was the first intergovernmental body with these more general terms of reference.

David Lubin, the founder of the IIA, was an American who had experienced at first hand the human misery which the economic depression inflicted on farmers in the 1890's and who in consequence became fired with a passionate determination to provide them with effective machinery at the international level for bettering their lot. By single-mindedness and persistence he persuaded ministers in the governments of several leading countries to heed his ideas, above all the King of Italy, so that, despite many set-backs, the institution which he had envisaged became reality in Rome in 1905 and started on a long and useful career not seriously interrupted till the period of World War II.

David Lubin saw and understood the weaknesses of

agriculture. He realized farmers' disabilities in the acquisition of technical knowledge and their lack of economic bargaining power. He realized too, which at that time few other people did, that national governments could make good these shortcomings to only a limited extent, however energetic their agricultural programmes. He perceived the need for international action by governments in certain classes of problems and for a permanent international secretariat to sustain and inform that activity. His insight and his achievement in getting his views accepted, at least in large part, in official quarters were the more noteworthy when it is remembered that at that date the world was considered to be running itself quite nicely with little or no regulation. It was a period when faith in the enterprise of private individuals and the self-regulating market stood at its zenith.

The IIA embarked upon what for those days was a bold programme of meetings and publications. It acted as the convening agency and often, too, as the secretariat for a whole series of scientific congresses. In part these were convened to initiate joint action by governments in respect of some international problem; it might be to co-ordinate some pest or disease control programmes and thus augment their effectiveness, or it might be a more modest objective such as to agree on the nomenclature for the classification of soils, or the use of certain standard weights and measures in agricultural statistics. The congresses served as forums for the exchange and dissemination of technical information; some gave rise to publications which served the same objective.

But the papers arising out of congresses constituted

only a small fraction of the IIA's publication activity, its programme for the collection, publication and distribution of information. It initiated, to mention but a few, the *International Yearbook of Agricultural Legislation*, a year-book and monthly bulletins of agricultural statistics, monthly bulletins of agricultural science and practice and of agricultural economics and sociology, international bibliographies on various subjects, international directories of institutions in various subject-fields, co-ordination and comparison of farm accountancy statistics, an international plant protection bulletin and an international year-book of forestry statistics. It prepared an impressive list of monographs on individual agricultural products, on farm credit, on co-operatives, on marketing of selected commodities, on agrarian reform, on farm household management, on the rural exodus, on agricultural co-operatives, on rural hygiene and many more. It initiated and organized the first World Census of Agriculture in 1930, this involving a number of preparatory meetings to secure as much common ground as possible in the questionnaires to be used and to reach agreement on definitions and statistical concepts. A second census planned for 1940 was only partially held because of the war and it was FAO which took up the tradition and organized the second full census in 1950.

The Institute operated under difficulties and its work suffered certain inevitable limitations and defects. Membership was drawn predominantly from European countries with only a handful from other continents; Asia, Africa and Latin America were sparsely represented. Not unnaturally therefore the Institute concentrated, at least in its special studies, on topics of interest to its European members, though even in these it made pioneering endeavours to achieve world-wide coverage of the subjects treated.

Too often it lacked financial and official support from its members. The fact that many governments got far in arrears with their contributions made it chronically short of funds. Further, some governments, instead of sending responsible high-level officials to IIA meetings and conferences, kept a permanent delegate at Rome, largely out of touch with his national government.

The Institute also encountered formidable difficulties in obtaining information for its publications. In those days the collection of agricultural statistics and the reporting of scientific research activities were still rudimentary in the majority of countries and almost non-existent in others. By meetings and visits, by persuasion and persistence, the Institute did much in a modest, unspectacular way to develop and improve national services in these fields in order that international compilations and comparisons might be made. The harvest is being reaped in the much more comprehensive series of data which FAO is able to publish today.

A further limitation stemmed from the then prevailing climate of international opinion, namely the absence of any services designed for the assistance of under-developed countries. On the one hand, very few under-developed countries prior to World War II had a voice and vote in the councils of nations; many that are now independent were still bound within colonial empires while, among the already independent, many were either insufficiently prosperous or insufficiently interested to send representatives. On the other hand, the more developed countries saw no advantage in and felt no obligation toward aiding the weaker ones. Metropolitan powers might or might not do little more than exploit commercially their dependent territories. But, compared with today, there was no widespread international sentiment for mutual aid; there lacked the stimulus of an ideological recruiting campaign and the enlarged prickings of the welfare conscience. As a result, the Institute was not used to purvey technical advice to any appreciable extent and did not direct attention specifically to the technical and economic problems of under-developed countries. Other strands of thought had to grow and be woven into the fabric before this type of activity obtained international recognition.

Indeed, up till 1914, so far as what is now called "the under-developed world" was concerned, competition with the West in regard to material progress had hardly commenced and the political significance of countries other than areas of European settlement had not become marked, with the single exception of Japan, whose successes in the Sino-Japanese War of 1894-95 and in the succeeding war with Russia had established a new respect for her powers and had started a train of doubt in the minds of other Asian nations about the inevitability of colonial dependency.

Moreover, up till 1914, the advanced nations were complacently operating both domestically and in international trade a well-oiled economic mechanism which produced such rapid expansion of production and trade that, in spite of the rapid rise in population, the prosperity of the individual steadily increased. The peoples of these countries, at least, believed in the inevitability of economic progress.

Events during World War I and the ensuing decade shattered these beliefs. The war had been won by the allied and associated powers only at fearful cost and only as a result of American intervention. It had strengthened the American economy but grievously weakened the European through loss of men and of wealth. International economic intercourse which had been suspended did not revive despite confident expectations of a return to normalcy; the export of capital was directed to unproductive purposes, international trade was bedevilled with quantitative restrictions while intercontinental movement of labour came to a standstill. Europe seemed to have lost her capacity for progress; she had certainly lost the lead.

Meanwhile, ideas current before 1914 about the rights of labour found much more vigorous expression. The Russian revolution put into violent practice the doctrines of equal opportunity and fair shares and strengthened the hand of less violent socialist or social-democratic movements in other countries. Concern as to labour questions expressed itself in the establishment, along with the League of Nations, of the International Labour Organisation (ILO), the first of what later have come to be called the "specialized agencies." The ILO set up a section to deal with agricultural labour, but was concerned primarily with hired and indentured labour — a very minor portion of the world's farm population. It had significance in that its dealings with indentured and plantation labour represented a first example of activity directed chiefly to aiding under-developed countries.

Also, the emergence of "welfare" thinking during the 'twenties and 'thirties in Europe, Australasia and last, but not least, the United States, under Roosevelt's first presidency, brought into prominent public discussion ideas as to the possible international application of the teachings which were gaining increasingly wide acceptance nationally. Something had to be done to aid the disadvantaged. The countries to which many people advocated offering wider economic opportunities were, by a curious and paradoxical twist of argument, Germany, Italy and Japan — nicknamed the "have-nots" on account of their lack of raw materials and colonies under their own flags. But when later rescued from this misdirection the sentiment was destined to have powerful consequences.

A decisive happening was the collapse in 1929 of the partially restored conventional economic system and the paralysis of industry and trade during the succeeding four years, during which unemployment in the industrialized countries rose to the fantastic figure of 40 millions. From the dire experiences of these black years dates general acceptance of the view that government is immediately as well as ultimately responsible for the maintenance of economic prosperity and for succouring those who fall victim to aberrations in the "system," another doctrine which is beginning now to be carried over to and applied in the international sphere.

The League of Nations, however, did rather little economic work in its early years. Compared with the spate of economic activity during the first decade of the United

Nations, the League concentrated on political issues and, apart from an interest in reparation and other financial problems, did not call a major economic conference until 1927, some eight years after its foundation. The League Secretariat made compilations of statistics relating to production, trade and finance, but, apart from initiating a series of figures on livestock products, a field which the International Institute of Agriculture had not touched, the League did nothing specific in agriculture; indeed many League members felt that the subject should be left in the hands of the IIA. The International Labour Office published one study: *Labour in Agriculture.*

At that time, in the 'twenties, no general statistics of food consumption existed, only a handful of family budget studies, while pronouncements as to optimum nutrition were as yet but whispers in research laboratories. Neither had anyone suggested publicly that technical advice be made available to under-developed countries; nor had any steps been taken to compare and discuss the international repercussions of governments' agricultural policies, in spite of the continuing disequilibrium in international trade. Agriculture remained one industry among many, less well served with statistics and so less reported on. Food was just a group of commodities.

The World Economic Conference of 1927 was followed by the great economic depression and hence by another gathering — the World Monetary and Economic Conference, held in London in 1933. The principal object of these meetings was to try to secure intergovernmental agreement for the reduction of tariffs, the abolition or reduction of quota restrictions on imports and the adoption of monetary policies to adjust and stabilize exchange rates, all of which it was hoped would lead to a recovery in international trade. The efforts were singularly unsuccessful.

However, during the 'thirties were established the *Centre international de sylviculture* to promote exchanges of technical information on sylviculture, the *Comité international du bois* to review the international trade in timber and to attempt to revive consumption; the International Wine Office for a similar purpose and the International Office for Epizootics.

Meanwhile, another movement of thought was beginning to come forward which was destined profoundly to affect agricultural policies. Behind the scientific curtain an increasing amount of work was being done in the fields of human and animal nutrition. In the nineteenth century nutrition could almost be classed with political economy among the dismal sciences, of interest only to a few university professors, but the dramatic discovery of the vitamins early in the present century brought it to life. It was established that certain diseases could be correlated with the lack of certain elements in the diet, and much concrete evidence was produced to show that good food is necessary to health. A newly-coined term "protective foods" denoted those which protected people against ill health and disease resulting from dietary deficiency. Correct feeding for expectant and nursing mothers and for infants was found greatly to reduce disease and mortality in these groups. Milk was singled out from among the common foods as the "protective food par excellence," richly provided with minerals and vitamins.

In 1935 these and other findings were published in a League of Nations Health Section report entitled *Nutrition and Public Health,* known as the "Burnet-Aykroyd Report."

Simultaneously, pioneering attempts were being made to measure the extent of malnutrition in some of the most developed countries. In the United States, a section of the Department of Agriculture organized the collection and analysis of family budget studies and attempted to correlate them with income. In the United Kingdom, Sir John Boyd Orr (now Lord Boyd-Orr) made a similar attempt using British data, and further tried to check his conclusions on consumption by income group against what was known as total national food supplies and of income distribution. The assertion in Sir John Boyd Orr's book *Food, Health, and Income* that two-thirds of the British people were malnourished hit the headlines. Soon afterwards the International Labour Office published a compendium of family budget material from all countries where such studies had been made, using this as the basis of a report with the significant title *Workers' Nutrition and Social Policy*. Such practical work on the diets of the people in America, Britain and elsewhere came at an opportune moment, for with the economic depression persisting and several millions of unemployed, various governments were under pressure to do more to alleviate the lot of those who through no fault of their own had been long without jobs. Yet governments were chary of increasing the rates of public relief in the form of cash handouts beyond a certain level. On the other hand, if further aid could be given in the form of a health protection programme supported by the best medical opinion, that would be more acceptable. In this way were born the "milk in schools" schemes in various countries and subsidies for cheap milk to expectant and nursing mothers. Nutritionists had at last drawn back the scientific curtain; their work was now of public interest and they were influencing government action.

This constitutes a practical illustration of the thesis advanced in Chapter II that new forms of organization and new government policies are required to give effect to the doctrines of the scientific and ethical revolutions. In this example people could not or would not spend money on the foods most valuable to their health and therefore there was a case for influencing their decisions by promoting "reduced price" schemes. On the ethical side the public felt unquestionably a degree of corporate responsibility for preventing extremes of poverty and malnutrition among fellow nationals, especially when these resulted not from individual indolence or fecklessness but from a break-down of the "system." The two motives in combination facilitated the significant departures in government policy in the 'thirties which laid the basis of the later concept of individual responsibility for ensuring that people are properly fed.

While these first steps were being taken, governments continued preoccupied with the consequences of the economic crisis. With the importing nations cutting down imports in an attempt to restore their financial "solvency," with food and raw material exporting countries not willing or not able to cut back primary production commensurately, huge stocks piled up. Millions of bags of coffee were burnt, enormous quantities of perishable food spoiled on farms for lack of markets, wheat was "denatured" (dyed red or blue) to prevent it being fed to human beings though it could still be used for animals. Simultaneously poor and unemployed people throughout the world lacked enough of the right sort of food to eat. Plenty in the midst of hunger.

Economic dislocation was especially severe in countries such as Argentina, Canada, Australia and New Zealand, the bulk of whose national income was derived from the sale of primary products to other countries. Export prices fell to one-quarter of their 1929 level and still goods could not move. Farmers piled up debts, many lost their farms and many of those who survived did so only by neglecting their soil and farmsteads. Small wonder that the representatives of these countries at the League of Nations were among the most active in seeking out ways to alleviate the crisis and get commodities moving again.

Prominent among those who saw a connection between the collapse of agricultural markets on the one hand and the emergence of public nutrition policies on the other was F.L. McDougall, Economic Advisor to the Australian High Commissioner in London. Unwanted surpluses could be used to promote health. The prosperity of the farmer could be restored by raising the nutrition and prosperity of the urban consumer, and the phrase "A marriage of health and agriculture" was coined. Conversely, if nation-wide demands for improved nutrition led to wider markets for agricultural products, the economic benefit to agriculture would be great and this would, in turn, be reflected in increased demands from the agricultural populations of the world for industrial products, thus, in the language of a certain constitution adopted ten years later, "contributing to an expanding world economy."

Accordingly, Stanley M. Bruce (Lord Bruce of Melbourne), Australian High Commissioner in London and representative at Geneva, decided early in 1935 to raise at the League of Nations the general issue of the relationship of nutrition to health, agriculture and economic problems. Great interest was aroused and the Council of the League was requested to appoint two committees — one of scientists to study the physiological problem of nutritional requirements and the other a mixed committee of scientists, agriculturalists and economists to prepare reports on the effects which the adoption by all nations of nutritional policies would have on health, agricultural development and international trade. Incidentally, Bruce, who happened to have the task of finding a chairman for the mixed committee, first approached Winston Churchill, who expressed great interest but, after taking some days to consider the matter, replied to the effect that his preoccupations with the mounting problems of defence made acceptance impossible. Lord Astor was therefore appointed.

Looking back now it is curious to observe that this important international committee thought of the nutrition problem largely in terms of the malnutrition prevailing in the more advanced countries. Its principal report *The Relation of Nutrition to Health, Agriculture and Economic Policy* does indeed contain short sections on nutrition in Asia and "colonial areas," but these were slender and uninformative. Among the committee's 21 members there was no representative from Asia, the Near East or Africa and only one from Latin America — an Argentinian. This was understandable on various counts. First, problems of nutrition in the under-developed countries had not yet been adequately studied. Secondly, it was only the governments of the wealthier countries which had sufficient public funds and adequate administrative machinery to launch nutrition policies. Thirdly, these countries were the principal customers of the primary producing countries, which hoped thus to move some of their agricultural surpluses into consumption.

The problem presented some obvious difficulties. Some of the principal surpluses — wheat, sugar, coffee and wine — could not be classed as protective foods. What the doctors were particularly recommending was more milk products, meat, vegetables and fruit. In fact, some governments devised surplus disposal programmes which had only partially a nutritional character; for example, the United States Government which had to deal at one and the same time with a large body of near-bankrupt primary producers and with millions of industrial unemployed, evolved a series of "Stamp Plans" not only for food but also for other products, such as cotton, through which surplus stocks of produce were distributed at bargain prices to needy groups. Twenty years later, when surplus disposal programmes again became a live issue, the same situation arose. Some surplus foods, such as skim milk powder, could readily be used to improve the quality of satisfactory diets; the distribution of others was less easy to defend on nutritional grounds.

The mixed committee reported in 1937 and concluded its summary with the following words:

> The malnutrition which exists in all countries is at once a challenge and an opportunity; a challenge to men's consciences and an opportunity to eradicate a social evil by methods which will increase economic prosperity.

The report proved a bestseller among League publications; it not merely attracted wide attention, it also provoked action. Within a year, 20 governments had implemented the recommendation to establish national nutrition committees which would advise governments on the formulation of nutrition policies. As to the other aspect, it cannot be claimed that the work of the mixed committee resulted in any agricultural surpluses being moved into consumption; in the period 1937-39 surpluses were disappearing for other reasons — general recovery of consumer purchasing power and preparations for war.

But this work had other far-reaching consequences. As Alexander Loveday, then Director of the Economic and Financial Section of the League Secretariat, said:

> The nutrition campaign seems to me to be of paramount importance not only on account of its immediate object, which is to improve the standard of living, but on account of the influence it is likely to have on our whole economic outlook. Ever since the time of Adam Smith economic thought has centred round the art of production or the conditions of citizens as producers. The nutrition movement reflects the first serious endeavour, certainly on an international scale, to consider the economics not of production but of consumption.

The second point that I want to mention is somewhat similar. Economists have concentrated in the past on problems of production. Production of what? Production of an endless series of inanimate objects. Those concerned with this nutrition campaign say: ' No, what you should really try to produce first is the best possible human beings — the best possible citizens.'

It signified a shattering of the entrenched belief that the play of prices in the market could and would automatically maintain a desirable equilibrium between production and consumption. It signified a victory for the view that in certain circumstances and certain fields well-being could be promoted by some degree of guidance by government and gave new impetus to the great debate which is still with us as to how much intervention there should be and what form it should take. Public opinion had been reluctant to recognize a need for influencing consumption, planning production and regulating trade; and, understandably, since these were fields in which over-control could do as much as undue laissez-faire to damage productivity and impede economic expansion. And even to apply a moderate amount of control proves difficult; satisfactory techniques have still to be acquired. But it was already then becoming apparent that to achieve the benefits of new scientific knowledge, in this case the relation of nutrition to health, and in combination therewith to go further in the active pursuit of "fair shares," some purposive activity was needed, some thought-out nutritional and agricultural policies related to one another.

It might be supposed that at this point the stage was virtually set for FAO, but in fact there were still certain missing elements of importance. For one thing governments had little experience in administering policies of this kind and any conscious effort to integrate food with agriculture might have had to wait years had it not been for the outbreak of war. Moreover, the desirability of new *international* machinery was certainly not seen.

Another aspect missing in the Geneva period was any advocacy of an expansion in agricultural production or any recognition that new arrangements might have to be devised to speed the adoption in farming of the latest knowledge of the agricultural scientists. This was perhaps natural enough since the existence of burdensome agricultural surpluses was one of the origins of the Geneva debate and since it could not be expected that the adoption by governments of positive nutrition policies could, for a time at least, stimulate consumption on such a scale as would turn those surpluses into shortages.

More surprisingly the mixed committee had little to say about the expansion of world population and the task of feeding it. Clearly the neo-Malthusians were not yet articulate. No one quoted "one hundred thousand new mouths a day" (or whatever the then figure was) and either doubted that they could be fed or urged an agricultural revolution to accomplish it. In part this was because the study of population statistics was only just being refined in the advanced countries — concepts of net reproduction rates, differential fertility and so on — and such studies as had been made suggested that the population in highly industrialized countries was likely to *decrease* during the present century. For the remaining two-thirds of the world, neither statistics nor even estimates could be presented. There lacked the empirical data for any cogent argument. In part it was the usual tendency of people to take the short view and, in a period of relative over-production and under-consumption, to be impressed by the apparent shortage of consumers rather than to fear a surplus of them. It is however idle to speculate on when these ideas might have intruded themselves if the Geneva initiatives had had an opportunity to develop in a world at peace.

Came the war. It is the common historical experience that wars are forcing grounds for new ideas and World War II was no exception. For all the belligerents and some of the neutrals, economic life was disrupted on a scale quite unprecedented. The almost insatiable demands of the war machine, giving rise to shortages in so many sectors, created massive problems of finance, production, labour supply, transportation and consumption, for all of which solutions had to be found. Because the amount of resources to be diverted to the war effort was greater than in World War I and because governments wished to avoid the mistakes of the previous occasion and in particular to arrange a more equitable distribution of sacrifices, the economies of most belligerent countries were brought under comprehensive control.

In the field of food consumption the vast food requirements of the armed forces, coupled with some inevitable falling off in food production and/or imports, quickly created shortages that could only be met by general rationing. Immediately here some of the newly-formed national nutrition committees were able to perform a service. They suggested dividing the population into categories according to nutritional requirements — light workers, heavy workers, expectant and nursing mothers, infants, children by age-groups. — and providing through rations a diet tailored to the needs of each group. These policies, which were widely adopted, not merely effected a substantial saving of supplies by withholding certain types of food from classes of consumers who did not need them but, more important, maintained and in some countries improved the nutritional status and health of the population. Despite many adverse factors, including women working in factories, air raids, congested transport and restricted medical facilities, the infant and maternal mortality rates actually fell in some belligerent countries. All this provided a convincing, conclusive demonstration that nutritional policy was no mere scientific theory but administratively applicable and fruitful in results. The nutritionists had in two or three years won recognition which without the war might have taken them as many decades to win.

In the sphere of distribution valuable lessons were also learned. Governments recognized, as they had barely begun to do toward the end of World War I, that, if supplies of a commodity were short, then either it must be rationed physically or its price must be permitted to rise to secure rationing by the purse. Price control without rationing would lead to wholesale evasion of regulations and other undesirable practices. Since on general policy grounds steep rises in the cost of living and consequential ones in wages were to be avoided, this meant that for all essential foods in short supply the distribution had to be by rationing accompanied by controlled prices.

By analogy, similar techniques had to be employed as between the allied powers in handling their internationally traded goods. The domestic price stabilization programmes would have been thwarted if, for instance, Britain and the United States had by competing against each other driven up the price of, say, peanuts in West Africa. As the war progressed, various boards were set up to co-ordinate overseas purchasing and to recommend international allocation of commodities in short supply. For foodstuffs the Combined Food Board was established with the United States, Canada and the United Kingdom as members. The Combined Raw Materials Board handled agricultural requisites such as feeding-stuffs and fertilizers. The experience gained by these bodies in administering international allocation programmes proved invaluable after the war to the International Emergency Food Council in dealing with even graver shortages.

In the sphere of food production the principal object was either to maintain output, as in Nazi-occupied Europe, or to expand it without any increase in labour supply or any large increase in prices. It was a long time, 15 years or more, since there had been any incentives to expanding agricultural production; the recent pressures had been all the other way. In South America and Australasia there was not much call for more output because the long shipping haul precluded the lifting of large supplies. In Britain a vigorous effort did produce an increase if production be measured in calories, because, by price fixing and subsidies, the government provoked a switch from luxury to basic food-stuffs. It was in Canada and the United States that a dramatic expansion in agricultural output was achieved which helped to victual Britain, kept supplied the vast American armed services and later, after war-end, provided the bulk of the relief to hungry Europe.

In the United States the strong demand for food at favourable prices provided the occasion for large-scale re-equipment of farms and the speedy adoption of the most advanced farming practices. Between the beginning and end of World War II American farmers acquired 50 percent more tractors, doubled their use of chemical fertilizer and increased food production by a third albeit with 12 percent fewer hands. In part this represented reaping the fruit of the Agricultural Adjustment, Soil Conservation, Farm Security and other programmes initiated before the war under the New Deal. In part it resulted from new efforts and even new discoveries during the war itself. In part it was the weather; a succession of good years without droughts or dust storms.

This achievement had repercussions far beyond the supplying of food to allied and liberated countries. It convinced Americans that the application of science and technology to agriculture could obtain results as startling as those obtained in industry. Not for them the "slow continuous epic of the soil" but rather the commando approach, namely that shock tactics and fine equipment could overcome any obstacle. Hurry was the order of the day. Once, shortly after the war, a farm near Washington, D.C. was "remodelled" in one day as a conservation demonstration — fields shaped and contoured, drains laid, windbreaks planted, crops drilled, farm buildings and homes redesigned and rebuilt.

During and after the war American servicemen were stationed in many countries and those who came from farm backgrounds were astonished at what they saw. They could not understand why farming in certain parts of Europe and still more in the under-developed countries should be so apparently primitive; draught animals instead of tractors, laborious manual methods, low-yielding varieties of crops, disease-ridden livestock and land tenure systems that denied the cultivator the benefits arising from his improvements. Here, they reasoned, was a golden opportunity to demonstrate what "modernization" could accomplish, if only they could get the job of bringing these people up to date.

And it was so to be. The United States, which before the war had still been comparatively isolationist in sentiment and largely aloof from events in other continents, now at the end of this war found itself called upon to provide relief, to save millions of people from starvation; and, because no other country could help on a sufficient scale and because the call could not go unanswered, the United States with her characteristic impulsive generosity did the job partly directly, partly through the United Nations Relief and Rehabilitation Administration (UNRRA). Relief, as we shall see, was soon replaced by financial aid, and financial aid was soon considered unsound unless supplemented by technical aid. That, in brief, is how American farm experts got started in the under-developed countries. Their passionate conviction that science has now made it possible to transform the oldest and slowest of human occupations is something wholly new in the world.

Agriculture here and throughout this essay must be taken to have a very wide meaning. The movement we are describing covered also that other source of food supply — the sea with its fisheries and their multifarious problems; likewise non-food products of the soil, especially fibres and wood (fuel, lumber, pulp) which provide clothing and shelter. Here, too, the techniques of production can be transformed to obtain the larger output required as living standards rise. Moreover, as FAO experts subsequently emphasized, there should be an intimate relationship between forest and agricultural policies in the spheres of land use and soil management. But we are running ahead of our story.

The next phase up to the establishment of FAO has been aptly told by Gove Hambidge in *The Story of FAO*;[1] the McDougall memorandum, written at an International Wheat Agreement meeting in Washington in 1942, its getting into the hands of Mrs. Roosevelt, McDougall's dinner at the White House, a period of silence, and then President Roosevelt's summoning of a Conference on Food and Agriculture in 1943 at Hot Springs, Virginia; the setting-up by that Conference of an Interim Commission which, during the two succeeding years, drafted the Constitution and determined the functions of the new organization and finally the birth of the Organization — FAO — at Quebec in October 1945.

To say that the whole of this decisive phase drew its main inspiration from the Geneva reformers on the one hand and from American faith in modern technology on

---

[1] GOVE HAMBIDGE, *The Story of FAO* (New York; D. Van Nostrand Company, 1955).

the other is no doubt an over-simplification, but sufficiently near the truth.

The Geneva inspiration was already apparent in the title of the Conference: "Food and Agriculture," a significant linking of consumers with producers. During the Conference discussions and in the Final Act nutrition policies took foremost place, followed by consequential observations on the raising of consumer purchasing power and maintaining an expanding world economy. Nutrition provided eight out of the first nine resolutions of the Conference. It was the point of departure and the *terminus ad quem*.

The American contribution and inspiration were derived from her own heartening experiences in applying to agriculture the latest findings of the organic sciences and of engineering. It had recently been summed up dramatically by President Roosevelt himself in his "Four Freedoms" speech which set out unequivocally the allies' war aims and included as a perfectly attainable target through modernization of agriculture the provision of enough food for all people in all lands. The nutritionists' goal could be reached through agricultural science. This shifted the emphasis, decisively and for several years to come, away from surplus disposal (a Geneva preoccupation) to expansion of food production, naturally enough in the prevailing wartime atmosphere of shortages; and it also for the first time focussed attention on the poorest and hitherto neglected peoples of the world, not merely the malnourished in the advanced countries but the far more numerous malnourished in Asia, Africa and Latin America. Thus the Americans were not content with defining nutritional targets, they believed they could be achieved within a finite period and that to do so an agricultural revolution should be spread around the world through the good offices of a new intergovernmental agency.

At last all the ingredients were to hand for the building of FAO. The ideas had taken some 50 years to come together and crystallize but the lineage was unmistakable. Atwater in his laboratory and David Lubin lobbying heads of governments, each unknown to the other but each starting rivers of development which were destined to converge into a single powerful philosophy and action agency. It had taken many years of patient, fruitful work on the one hand by nutrition workers learning more about their science and on the other by the International Institute of Agriculture developing the habit and some of the techniques of intergovernmental action. It had required the imagination and zeal of the Geneva reformers and a world in economic perplexity to listen to them. It had required finally the dramatic leadership of a great President rising above the tumult of a devastating world war.

It remained only for the Interim Commission to clothe in suitable words this far-reaching new endeavour and with this preamble to its Constitution FAO could begin work:

> The Nations accepting this Constitution, being determined to promote the common welfare by furthering separate and collective action on their part for the purposes of
>
> > raising levels of nutrition and standards of living of the peoples under their respective jurisdictions,

securing improvements in the efficiency of the production and distribution of all food and agricultural products,

bettering the condition of rural populations,

and thus contributing toward an expanding world economy,

hereby establish the Food and Agriculture Organization of the United Nations, hereinafter referred to as the "Organization," through which the Members will report to one another on the measures taken and the progress achieved in the fields of action set forth above.

CHAPTER IV

FORMATIVE INFLUENCES: SHORTAGES, POPULATION GROWTH AND UNDER-DEVELOPED COUNTRIES

The great decision had been taken, and for once first things had been put first. Food — the essential of life; Agriculture — the occupation of two-thirds of the population of the world; all the consumers and the majority of producers vitally concerned about what might be achieved in this field.

The Chairman of the First Session of the FAO Conference, Lester B. Pearson of Canada (now Minister of External Affairs), stressed the novelty of the experiment in his Introduction to the *Conference Report*:

> The first of the new, permanent United Nations agencies is now launched. There are few precedents for it to follow; it is something new in international history. There have been functional international agencies with more circumscribed objectives and tasks, but FAO is the first which sets out with so bold an aim as that of helping nations to achieve freedom from want. Never before have the nations got together for such a purpose.
>
> FAO will bring the findings of science to the workers in food and agriculture, forestry and fisheries everywhere; and

it will bring the practical problems of these workers everywhere to the attention of the scientists. It will assemble, digest and interpret information to serve as a basis for the formulation of policy, national and international. It can suggest action, but only through the activites of governments themselves can the objectives be finally won.

FAO was new because its concept was bolder, its terms of reference more vigorous. It was to be an "action agency."

It is worth pausing to consider what we mean by this term, so much used and abused, and in its literal sense so misleading. It is not a federal or even confederal government; it possesses hardly any legislative or executive powers; it cannot compel. And yet it is different from the pre-war agencies. Whereas they confined themselves on the one hand to providing facilities for inter-governmental discussion and on the other to publication of fact-finding reports, the new agencies are used by governments as means through which they themselves take action — generally of two main kinds: first, recommendations to themselves and each other that certain specified action be undertaken, and, secondly, the obtaining of experts and equipment to help develop their national programmes. But although this represents a much more positive use of international machinery than ever before, it still rests with governments to make much or little use of the new facilities; the degree to which the name "action agency" is justified depends on the extent to which governments agree to take action through the machinery of that agency.

Lester Pearson perceived this at Quebec. In his peroration to the proceedings of that Conference he said:

FAO is, in the last analysis, people and governments. So it remains for us, the people, to make this Organization a success. I have no doubt of the competence and zeal of the Organization itself under its great Director-General. I have some fear, however, that the governments, because of apathy or ignorance, may not give FAO the support it must have, may not implement its recommendations or accept its advice. I can only hope that my fears in this respect will be entirely groundless, and that say, five years from now, when I take up the long list of recommendations which we have now accepted as a guide for sound action, I will be able to see written after each one: ' Action already taken by FAO and its Member Governments.'

Pearson's fears had some justification for there was no unanimity among governments as to how FAO should be used. At one extreme, stood those in whose view FAO should be no more than an intelligence service, assembling information, digesting and publishing it; at the other extreme, those who would make it a legislature and trading house combined; and there were all shades of opinion in between. These conflicts of view were to show up in many of the issues debated at FAO during the next few years.

Although these struggles constitute a major formative influence in the growth of any international agency, it is considered, for some obscure reason, indecent to refer to them. This prudery is surely a mistake. Differences of view are of the stuff of democratic life; only in a totalitarian world would governments be all of one mind as to the functions of international agencies. We should welcome variety in governments' attitudes and policies and enjoy the effort involved in arriving at the compromises which enable democratic institutions to work. At the least we should be well advised to face up frankly to these differences since they will continue to be a permanent feature of international life.

At Hot Springs, during the work of the Interim Commission, and at Quebec there were some delegations who took the view that FAO should be just a bigger and better International Institute of Agriculture, performing a valuable, and respectable, service in collecting and disseminating information. Several wanted FAO to be an action agency in the sense defined above; and these included not only under-developed countries but also some of the wealthier primary-producing countries.

The field in which at Hot Springs and subsequently action was expected and desired as distinct from "consultation" was that of international commodity arrangements. While there was much talk of improving nutrition and modernizing agriculture, these were at that time regarded by all but a few as programmes which each government could frame for itself; the "get together" was envisaged chiefly for commodity agreements and at Hot Springs alternative commodity control techniques were hotly debated. Though opinions differed as to what could be done, there was agreement on the aim, namely stabilization of prices of internationally traded commodities without resort to restriction of trade.

At Quebec these ideas received less attention, for the United States Government had just published its sketch plan for an International Trade Organization to which, in the view of the United States and other leading delegations, all commodity control matters would properly belong.

However, the election of Sir John Boyd Orr as Director-General made it certain, wittingly or unwittingly, that the attempt to become an action agency would be made first in the field of international trade. Though Sir John was a scientist and scholar, his overwhelming interest was in economic and financial questions. His personal inclination was reinforced by public pressures arising out of the food crisis which spread across the world after the cessation of hostilities.

Within six months of election he was calling a meeting to promote international allocation of food-stuffs in short supply and secured the establishment of the International Emergency Food Council, IEFC (May 1946). This was action and it met a felt need. But, while the more conservative powers felt constrained to concede the smaller powers a voice in the allocation of scarce foods, they were worried at the prospect of FAO getting into the action field and succeeded in keeping the IEFC and its Secretariat organizationally separate.

Before the end of his first year of office, Sir John went further and launched his World Food Board proposal, one of the most ambitious designs for international action ever put forward. In doing so, he aligned himself with those who wanted FAO to be a trading agency and a finance house in addition to its other functions. Most of FAO's second year of life was spent in examining these proposals and rejecting them at the Third (Geneva) Session of the Conference. Six months later Sir John retired and Norris E. Dodd became Director-General. Whatever his disappointments in the economic financial field, Sir John had given the new organization dynamic leadership when most needed and had laid, as will be seen, a firm foundation of technical activities in FAO's programme which was to have great significance later on.

Dodd's personal interests lay in very different directions, but the radicals among Member Governments were not yet ready to admit defeat. Although by the crop year 1948/49 the world food shortage was considerably eased, the available supplies which deficient countries needed lay in the dollar area and importing countries were short of dollars. Moreover, it was becoming unlikely that the Havana Charter would be accepted and an International Trade Organization established. Hanging their request on the peg of currency difficulties they called at a FAO Council meeting for yet another study of the problem, in response to which a panel of experts convened by the Director-General produced proposals for an International Commodity Clearing House. This in turn was rejected and the subject firmly sent to bed by the establishment of a Committee on Commodity Problems.

The story of how FAO dealt first with shortages and then with surpluses will be examined more closely in the next chapter. Unfortunately, the crises developed long before anyone was ready. It was one thing to engage at Hot Springs in leisurely debate as to the relative merits of quota or Keynesian buffer-stock schemes for commodity control; it was quite another to secure agreement among governments as to particular prices and particular quantities of a particular commodity; witness the years of negotiations before governments concluded an International Wheat Agreement. And it proved quite impossible to agree on practicable procedures for an international agency which would buy and stock and sell commodities in all sorts of currencies on a scale which would significantly ameliorate world shortages and surpluses. Some hard thinking had been done but far from enough to define the parameters of the problems involved. That process of thinking and of breaking down the problems into manageable segments is still going on most usefully in the Committee on Commodity Problems.

While much of FAO's energy was concentrated on international trade problems during the years 1946 to 1948, nonetheless a beginning was being made on establishing an intelligence service and on developing a wide range of technical activities in the fields of agriculture, nutrition, fisheries and forestry. These activities soon took a variety of forms — organizing international meetings of experts on a particular problem, e.g. grain storage; bringing governments together to take concerted action, e.g. rinderpest control; helping governments to obtain equipment and materials, e.g. certain vaccines and insecticides which at the time were still scarce; sending missions to advise governments on specific problems or sending individual experts for an extended period.

Without doubt this technical work would in any case have grown steadily and would have become a major feature of the Organization's programme. It met a felt need, it embraced a vast subject field — from land reform to fishing gear, from systemic insecticides to forest fires — and it seldom involved political issues. But it was destined to receive a powerful impetus and to acquire a new context and new significance as the result of pressures of public opinion which were coming to demand a type of international activity later called "Technical Assistance." However, in order to understand how the Technical Assistance idea emerged we must first pick up certain other strands of international thought.

One of the influences which swung FAO on to the new path was a growing public interest in the population problem, a feeling among peoples and governments that much more energetic action would be needed to expand food production in face of the substantial expansion of population. The study of world population trends is a development of the last ten years, and this for two reasons. It was not until just before and during the war that techniques of measuring rate of increase — "net reproduction rate" and so on — were effectively worked out, and it was not until after the war that serious efforts were made to use (and hence to improve) the statistical data of the under-developed countries.

In the late 1930's there was not any great concern with world population factors. Indeed, it was then very generally felt that in the more developed countries the fall in the birth-rate which had been characteristic of the inter-war period might be dangerous and might lead to a decline in the political significance of countries where this phenomenon was particularly marked.

During World War II the attitude towards the population problem was not markedly changed. As a result, between 1943 and 1945, those concerned with the postwar problems of food and agriculture did not place any particular importance upon the matter. Here the change between 1945 and 1955 has been very great.

In the highly developed countries the years immediately following the war saw a very marked increase in birth-rates. The birth-rate figures for France increased from 15.1 per 1,000 in 1937 to 21.1 per 1,000 in 1948. The increase in the United Kingdom and Scandinavia, although not so steep, was marked, while in the United States, Canada, Australia and New Zealand, the increase was much greater. These increases were, however, regarded by most demographers as being a result of the repatriation of the demobilized and the phenomenon was referred to as "the baby boom." It was anticipated that once this period, during which postponed marriages were consummated, was over, the birth-rate figures would return to the declining pattern of the 1920's and 1930's. There has been some tendency in this direction in Europe, although in 1953 birth-rates in most countries were at substantially higher levels than in 1937. However, in the United States, Canada, Australia and New Zealand, no tendency towards any significant decline in birth-rates had occurred up to 1954. In the United States population is actually increasing at the rate of two and a half millions a year.

Infant mortality statistics in most countries for which reasonably accurate information is available show that in the last 30 years the rates have halved and in a number of cases, particularly among highly developed countries, have fallen by over 60 percent.

Turning to the under-developed countries, little change occurred in birth-rates, but the adoption of better methods of hygiene and of the control of diseases, including for instance malaria, resulted in a most spectacular fall in death-rates. It can therefore be claimed that over the last two decades quite extraordinary progress has been made in what may be described as death control. While the complete accuracy of the statistics of some of the under-developed countries may be doubted, figures such as the following are no doubt largely accurate. Comparing the death-rate figures for 1937 and 1953, those for Ceylon fell from 21.7 per 1,000 to 10.9; for Chile, from 23.1 to 13.2; for Mexico, from 24.4 to 15; for Venezuela, from 18.1 to 9.9. There are few under-developed countries in which a striking fall in death-rates has not taken place. In these matters the World Health Organization is taking vigorous and effective action.

The success of death control obviously means that expectation of life is increasing in the under-developed world, but few accurate statistics on this factor exist. In the more highly developed world the last two decades have shown a considerable lengthening of life expectancy and in general it may be said that since the middle 'thirties some five to six years have been added to the expectation of life in North America and Western Europe.

In preparation for the World Population Conference held at FAO Headquarters, Rome, in September 1954, the Population Division of the United Nations prepared important papers on the actual and estimated populations of the world by continents, by regions and by countries. Assuming the median rate adopted for these purposes, world population at the end of 1955 would be 2,600 millions and by 1970 would be 3,150 millions, or a rate of increase of 1.47 percent per annum. This means that during the present year the population of the world will be increasing at the rate of 100,000 persons per day. The gradual appreciation of the significance of the rapid rate of population growth is one of the major factors that must affect world thinking and the attitude of governments towards the problems of food and agriculture during the next decade.

FAO first drew attention to the subject and to its implications for food supply in its first *World Food Survey* (1946); to calculate the additional amount of food the world would need to achieve certain nutritional targets by 1960, it had to make assumptions about world population at that date. It showed that, compared with 1935-39, the 1960 food supplies of the under-developed countries would have to be up by 35 percent merely to maintain pre-war consumption levels, and by 90 percent to achieve the nutritional targets for the enlarged population.

Meanwhile people were meditating upon the economic implications of the data now being published in large quantities by the demographic experts of the United Nations. It was remarked that, whereas in Europe during the nineteenth century a rapid growth in population was outstripped by the still more rapid growth of national income, now in the under-developed countries population and national income were expanding at about the same pace so that there was no appreciable improvement in income *per caput*. From this it was argued that much greater efforts would have to be made to augment production in these countries and this argument in turn branched out in a variety of directions — proposals for stimulating at the national level savings and investment, proposals for stepping up the volume of international lending through the International Bank for Reconstruction and Development and other bodies, proposals for stabilizing international trade and proposals for making available technical advice to modernize agriculture and establish new industries.

In that part of this great debate which concerned agriculture two strikingly opposed schools of thought emerged: the neo-Malthusians who argued that Malthus was right after all and the "optimists" who held that man's ingenuity would prevail. The Director-General of FAO put the two views aptly in his report for 1951/52. He said:

> Many sincere people do not believe the world can possibly feed this rapidly growing population. They argue that the amount of food we can produce from soil and sea is more or less static. We have not reached the limit, but there is not very much room for expansion. If humanity is not to be starved out, therefore, we must cut population growth by deliberately reducing the birth-rate as widely and effectively as we are reducing the death-rate. The population has to be tailored to fit the food supply rather than the other way round.
>
> Other people believe just as sincerely that the earth's natural resources are sufficient to produce an adequate food supply for the world's growing population if we make full scientific use of those resources. They also argue that there are bound to be many more discoveries and advances that will help to increase world food production, some perhaps a great deal.
>
> There are all shades of opinion in between.

And on another occasion in the same year he said:[1]

> They (the neo-Malthusians) may be right. I don't know what the distant future may hold. I do know that we have to live through the present to reach any future, and we aren't

---

[1] Lecture at Pacific University, Oregon, April 1952.

doing as well in the present as we can do...... I have enough faith in my kind to believe that we will not give up to hunger — now or in some dim future — until we have tried everything we can think of. We haven't done that yet even on a small scale, let alone all over the world, all together.

That was the spirit in which, under Dodd's leadership, Member Governments in FAO dealt with the impact on food and agriculture of the world population problem.

These matters cannot be thought of merely in global terms; they have to be considered, as they have to be tackled by each people within its own borders. Each country knowing that with every decade it will need larger and larger supplies of food has either to produce the additional supplies at home or import them from abroad, and in the latter case will have to pay for expanded imports by expanded exports of other goods and services. Such a choice does not nowadays altogether settle itself by the free play of prices and the free movement of men and goods across frontiers. So many protective devices have been built into national economies that automatic adjustment no longer takes place; governments have increasingly to regulate or plan their foreign trade in relation to domestic production, and this goes as much for those countries which face shortages as those which find themselves with surpluses. Without doubt some countries face far graver pressure of population on existing resources than others; some have to invest far larger amounts of capital to obtain a similar increase in production. In these most disadvantaged countries, not able if they were willing to use the safety-valve of emigration, *per caput* income can grow only more slowly than elsewhere unless some unforeseen change takes place in the exploitability of resources, e.g. the discovery of oil or the application of atomic energy. Such progressive falling behind in the cavalcade of progress will not these days be lightly tolerated and, as the problem becomes more apparent, pressures are likely to build up to find some international solutions, though along what lines it is not yet possible to discern.

Had it come alone, the population problem would not have made such an explosive entrance on to the post-war stage. It gained in dramatic strength because it was accompanied by the emergence of the under-developed countries as a political force.

In the days of the League of Nations, the countries of Asia, the Middle East and Africa were largely under the political control of the metropolitan powers, with the result that most of them were not directly represented at the League. One of the consequences was that the views of this great mass of more than half the world's population were not brought to the attention of League members. Nor did the great group of Latin American countries participate as fully in the League's work as they have done in the United Nations. Intergovernmental consultation in those days was primarily between European governments plus certain overseas countries and territories engaged in producing food and raw materials for the European market.

References in international discussions to "backward" or "less developed" countries almost always meant the countries of Eastern and South-eastern Europe; the Bosporus seemed the limit of the intellectual horizon. The export of European capital to other continents, so massive prior to 1914, had diminished to a trickle; and of that still moving the greater part went into ventures producing exports for Europe — mines, plantations, oil-wells.

The invitations to Hot Springs threw a wider net and out of 44 countries represented 27 might be classed as under-developed; the majority of these were Latin American. South-east Asia remained colonial and silent.

At the end of the war, international aid — economic, financial and technical — was made available it is true on an unprecedented scale through the United Nations Relief and Rehabilitation Administration (UNRRA), but it was directed to war-torn countries which, except for China, the Philippines and Ethiopia, meant Europe and the Near East. Great have been the changes between 1945 and 1955. The most significant date was perhaps 1947 when the British withdrew from the Indian subcontinent bringing into existance two great new sovereign states, India and Pakistan, both destined to have weighty influence in international affairs. Other new faces at the international conference tables included Ceylon, Burma, Indonesia, Korea, Egypt, Syria, Lebanon, Byelorussia and the Ukraine.

Of the present members of the United Nations not less than 40 out of 60 are under-developed in the roughly accepted meaning of that term. In FAO membership the proportion is 49 out of 71. One practical result is an insistence in the debates of the United Nations and the specialized agencies upon attention to the needs of Asia, the Middle East, Latin America and, in some degree Africa, and that when the under-developed countries wish to act together they can command a majority in the general assemblies and sometimes also in the executive councils or governing bodies of the international organizations.

Delegations from under-developed countries are rightly not slow to point out the contrasts between the living standards of their peoples and those of more developed countries. According to estimates made by the United Nations Secretariat, there is only one country with national per caput income of over 1,500 dollars and only two others with more than 1,000 dollars. A considerable number of countries in Europe and Australasia have figures of 700 to 800 dollars. On the other hand, per caput incomes in the greater part of the under-developed world range from 50 to 100 dollars.

Moreover, the situation is getting worse inasmuch as the rich are getting richer faster than the poor are. The United Nations *World Economic Report* for 1952 stated:

> Studies in recent years indicate that while world income has grown rapidly, it is now even more unequally distributed among countries than in the period immediately preceding the second world war and the last two or three years have done little to alter this general picture of a widening gap between rich and poor countries.

A comparison between 1948 and 1953 indicates that in North America the national per caput income has increased by several hundred dollars and in the other more highly developed countries by 100 or more dollars. This means that the increases achieved in the highly developed world are substantially greater than the total per caput income in most of the under-developed world.

Here, it can be argued, is a gigantic social and economic problem crying out for remedies. And the governments of the developed countries have indeed some conscience in the matter. At the national level the state is largely committed to mitigating poverty arising out of inequality of opportunity and beyond this it undertakes through taxation to redistribute income on a massive scale. Representatives of under-developed countries naturally make use of the analogy and urge that the principles and policies adopted within nations to reduce the extremes of wealth and poverty should be adopted likewise between nations.

The governments which advance these arguments at international meetings face at home a public opinion persistently clamouring for economic development. A significant proportion of their people have come to hear how the wealthier peoples live. They have seen films, read illustrated papers, talked with American and other military personnel, listened to radio, seen the new-fangled consumption goods purchased by their own well-to-do. They no longer regard these standards as unattainable; they expect their governments to deliver prosperity, and quickly too. Moreover they have votes and their impatience will not be denied. It threatens to eliminate caste systems, princes, ruling classes that appear to stand in the way.

Governments of these countries feel, in their turn, a heightened obligation to get something done. Many of them have taken over from former colonial powers and have to prove in the eyes of their citizens that they can do better than the former rulers. In other under-developed countries, where previously government occupied itself with the army and the foreign service, there is insistence from a broader-based public opinion that government should be more responsible for economic affairs and prosperity in general. All this adds up to an intense and continuing preoccupation with development proposals in the "have-not" countries.

How do the advanced countries react to these representations? They turn no deaf ear. They realize their involvement; indeed, the speed at which their public opinions have moved in the last ten years is something without precedent in history. They accept a share in the responsibility for bringing forward the under-developed countries. Of course this sentiment has not the strength that it has in matters of wealth and poverty at home; of course it is weak compared with the amount of effort that will in due time be needed at the international level; but it is there and is growing.

While at the more popular level this sentiment has chiefly a humanitarian content, among more sophisticated people it is strengthened by calculations of economic and political self-interest. On the economic side, it is not difficult to marshall arguments in support of developing production and purchasing power in the low-income countries since such policies will augment demand for the exports of advanced countries, maintain high levels of employment there, provide outlets for investment funds and increase the volume of international trade. One does better business with a prosperous neighbour than with a poor one. There is more trade between the United States and Canada than between the United States and the whole of Latin America.

On the political side the metropolitan powers are making unique efforts to bring development to their remaining dependent territories, partly at least to forestall unrest and revolt. Likewise, the advanced countries of the so-called western world have been stimulated by the ideological confiict with the U.S.S.R. to show that democratic capitalism works effectively and brings benefits to have-not countries. They have shown particular zeal to aid countries which appear to be still uncommitted between the two leading political philosophies.

With these divers considerations in mind the advanced countries have embarked upon an impressive series of efforts to provide aid. In 1946 the International Bank for Reconstruction and Development was established; in 1947 came the United States Marshall Aid Programme directed primarily toward Europe but in many aspects a practice swing before the big drive; in 1949 the Truman " Point Four " proposals, which led on the one hand to the economic aid administered directly by the United States Government which has spent thousands of millions of dollars over the past five years, and on the other to the United Nations Expanded Technical Assistance Programme (ETAP) with a budget of some 20 to 25 million dollars per annum; in 1950 the Colombo Plan for Co-operative Economic Development in South and South-east Asia in which the British Commonwealth territories and the United States came together to provide finance and equipment for the development schemes of less advantaged Commonwealth members in South-east Asia.

Before we continue the list, an important qualification should be made as to the United Nations Technical Assistance programme. This is far from being a one-sided transfer of aid from developed to under-developed countries. Although initiated by the United States and substantially supported as to finance and experts by the advanced countries it is a truly co-operative effort in which *all* nations contribute, each according to his means and ability. Some of the smallest countries have provided technical experts for service elsewhere.

To return to our list, a proposal has been worked out for the establishment of an International Finance Corporation (IFC) to be operated by the International Bank. The international financing activity of the International Bank is handicapped by the fact that its Articles of Agreement prevent it from granting loans without government guarantee as well as from making equity investments in participation with private capital. During the last General Assembly, the United States announced its intention of contribution to the IFC, and this organization is likely to become fully operative in the near future.

The 1954 session of the United Nations Assembly considered a proposal for establishing a Special United Nations Fund for Economic Development (SUNFED), a proposal which had been under discussion for some two years since a committee of nine experts reported [unanimously in favour of it. The proposal envisages a fund of 250 million dollars (with, presumably, further contributions to maintain the fund at that level) to be used to finance non-self-liquidating projects either by grants or by long-term interest-free loans. This plan has received warm approval from most of the under-developed countries but has so far not secured the support of those countries which would have been major contributors. The attitude of the United States, the United Kingdom, Canada, France and some other countries is that until a system of internationally supervised disarmament is brought into operation, they cannot provide the necessary resources to support the SUNFED proposals.

Looking back over the past decade the change in attitudes and in activity in the field of international aid has been nothing less than revolutionary. What is surprising is not that so much remains to be done — that will always be the case — but that so much has been set on foot in so short a time.

This change in the climate of international affairs has had immense significance for FAO. In the new climate FAO has been able to find tremendous support for its technical activity. While premature attempts to make FAO an action agency for internationally traded commodities failed, its present action programme is one which can grow just as fast as resources are made available for it, one which will remain in strong demand for the next decade and beyond, one which will gratifyingly strengthen the habit of intergovernmental co-operation.

During its first ten years of life FAO has been piloted through a turbulence of ideas far more violent than those which prevailed during its ante-natal days. At birth its functions represented a careful compromise between the conservative and radical schools. Almost immediately the world food crisis gave the radicals an opportunity to seek to revise the balance and get "teeth" put into the FAO Constitution or, alternatively, to establish some parallel agency with strong executive powers. While the Secretariat was coping with these demands it had also to build up what all governments wanted, namely, a comprehensive intelligence service. Despite distractions this was done and gives general satisfaction. No sooner had the shortage/surplus campaign died down, than the clamour for technical assistance became a roar; rudder hard over and services in the technical fields rapidly manned and extended.

The next chapters will examine FAO's achievements of the past decade under these three main headings: the valiant attempt to deal with shortages and surpluses, the building up of a fact-finding information service and the development of the technical activities of the Organization.

Chapter V

SHORTAGES AND SURPLUSES

World War II put an end to unemployment and to surpluses except in a few countries cut off from their traditional markets. It created full employment and shortages. But, while governments' main preoccupation was with shortages, the fear of surpluses recurring later was by no means exorcized.

The Hot Springs Conference reflected both trains of thought. It predicted at war-end a short-term period of shortages:

> There are likely to be not only severe shortages of the principal food-stuffs but shortages of transport, including shipping, and of the means of production, including fertilizers, seeds, machinery, farming implements, gasoline, etc.....
> The dominant problem in this short-term period will be..... planning the production programme on a realistic basis which puts the elimination of hunger first and the nutritional improvement of diet second..... It will be necessary to have international co-ordination to avoid monopolistic practices or an unrestrained competition for scarce supplies of food-stuffs, means of production and transport.....

It predicted, also accurately, that the shortages would give way to surpluses:

> The period of shortages will, in due course, come to an end, but, with the recovery of the devastated areas, coupled with intensified production elsewhere, there will be a danger of a situation occurring similar to that which followed the last war leading to over-production of cereals, sugar and other products, accompanied by a heavy fall in prices, with attendant losses and hardship to producers.

As to the shortages, it foreshadowed the need for an internationally representative body to allocate scarce supplies (Resolution XIII). As to surpluses, it prophecied the need for national agricultural adjustment programmes framed in the light of international review and consultation (Resolution XV) and beyond this it advocated international commodity agreements (Resolution XXV) and special international measures for wider food distribution (Resolution XXVII). Taken together, these recommendations constituted a surprisingly accurate forecast of what the world would need in the post-war decade — and some of which the world got.

By the time of the Quebec Conference, governments' plans for dealing with these various problems had taken more concrete shape. UNRRA had been created, so FAO was relieved of concerning itself with matters of relief and immediate rehabilitation. FAO should come into play as UNRRA fades out and should help governments plan their reorientation programmes as the period of shortages comes to an end.[1] Looking further ahead:

> It would be folly to disregard the possibility of surpluses developing, and FAO should study how to deal with such surpluses in the period before they appear.[2]

---

[1] *Report of the First Session of the FAO Conference*, p. 15.
[2] *Report of the First Session of the FAO Conference*, p. 37.

The Director-General accepted and acted on this recommendation with enthusiasm. But when the discussion turned to commodity agreements the governments issued a warning:

> In the economic field the forms of international collaboration in which FAO will be most directly concerned will in the main relate to matters which are the responsibility of other international organizations, particularly such organizations as may be set up to undertake responsibility for commercial and commodity policy.....
> In such matters FAO will work with and through other international bodies. [1]

Governments' intentions were clearly enough expressed: FAO was to keep off the short-term crisis and keep off commercial and commodity policy; it should concentrate on long-term issues of nutrition, production and (national) distribution.

The course of subsequent events and the personality of the Director-General did not smooth the way for evolution of FAO activity along the lines laid down at Quebec. The world food situation rapidly worsened and many became disposed to blame the agencies handling it — UNRRA, the Combined Food Board, and the Emergency Economic Committee for Europe. Impatience vented itself at the United Nations General Assembly the following February. Sir John Boyd Orr cabled: "FAO willing accept responsibility for mobilizing world resources to meet this crisis. As a first step we would propose calling conference earliest possible date....."

---

[1] *Report of the First Session of the FAO Conference*, p. 43.

The meeting took place in Washington, D. C. in May. Sir John had prepared a survey of the food situation expected in 1946/47, which showed that nine European countries would have less than 2,000 calories' worth of food available per head per day, barely two-thirds of their normal supply. Grain export availabilities were forecast at 20 million metric tons compared with minimum requirements of 30 million tons. Faced with these and other facts the meeting of governments recommended that the FAO Secretariat keep them appraised with quarterly bulletins on the situation, that bread-grain be milled to at least 85 percent extraction and mixed with 5 percent diluents, that fats be diverted from soap use and sugar from alcohol, that the Combined Food Board (United States, United Kingdom and Canada only) be broadened into IEFC with membership open to all countries having an important interest in any of the commodities under allocation, and finally that the Director-General submit to the next session of the FAO Conference proposals for dealing with the long-term problems including the risk of accumulating surpluses.

Governments had been galvanized into action by the crisis and the allocating machinery was widened and democratized. But governments adhered to their policy of keeping FAO out of the short-term tasks. The IEFC set to work on 1 July 1946, with a series of Commodity Committees and a Secretariat paid by FAO but separate and maintaining no particular contact with the FAO Secretariat in its daily work. Each committee recommended a division of the available export supply among the importers and these allocation recommendations passed out to governments through the Central Council were almost without exception acted upon. As supplies improved the committees one after another wound themselves up during 1947 and 1948. As the distinction between the emergency and long-term problems became more and more blurred, governments felt less objection and saw some economies in amalgamating IEFC work with that of FAO; accordingly, on 1 January 1948, the IEFC was dissolved and its Central Committee became the " International Emergency Food Committee " of the FAO Council and reported through it to the FAO Conference. The Secretariat, reduced in size, became the Distribution Division of FAO.

The IEFC, taking over and adapting to the critical situation the techniques developed by the Combined Food Board, achieved what governments unanimously regarded as an excellent performance. To quote the *Report of the Second Session of the FAO Council*:

> Had the allocation system not been operating during the period of extreme shortage, the world would have suffered an unrestricted scramble for food-stuffs, particularly cereals, the results of which might have been of the utmost seriousness.
> The work of IEFC has enabled governments to develop a pattern of co-operation in international action helpful to the objectives of FAO. It has enabled them to gather and co-ordinate a great deal of most valuable information about current supply and demand situations.

Its approach was truly objective in appraising the needs of countries even though in respect to certain commodities some governments may have had a considerable say. Moreover, it set a precedent in co-operation to secure fairer shares for all; the tradition and techniques which it established will be remembered and could be revived if ever again occasion should require such action.

As to the last recommendation of the Special Meeting on Urgent Food Problems in May 1946, the Director-General responded with alacrity to the invitation to produce proposals for new international functions to deal with long-term problems. His message was: " There never has been enough food in the world, " but science applied to agriculture could easily provide enough. " The limiting factor is not the physical capacity to produce enough food but the ability of nations to bring about the complex economic adjustments necessary to make adequate production and distribution possible. " He addressed himself to the nature of these adjustments. Producers were frustrated, he argued, by instability of markets and by insufficiency of consumer purchasing power. " Food, " he said, " is more than a trade commodity ; it is an essential of life. " He proposed a World Food Board which would :

1. stabilize prices by buffer stocks schemes ;
2. hold a world food reserve against famine ;
3. finance surplus disposal programmes to needy people ;
4. co-operate with a credit-issuing agency (to be created) ;
5. co-ordinate bodies dealing with individual commodities.

This was manifestly asking too much of governments. They would have to subscribe extremely large sums of money at a time when they needed every penny to restore or maintain their own solvency. In addition, they would be expected to part with sovereignty over a number of matters which they regarded as vital to the management of their own economies and their policies of full employment; and all this in favour of a scheme the practical operation of which had not been adumbrated in any way.

No wonder the Second Session of the FAO Conference at Copenhagen in September 1946 was non-committal about the plan. It set up a Preparatory Commission under the chairmanship of S. M. Bruce to examine the proposals but with much narrower terms of reference, namely how

> to develop and organize production, distribution and utilization of basic foods to provide diets on a health standard for the people of all countries, and to stabilize agricultural prices at levels fair to producers and consumers alike.

One of the most high-powered international seminars of ministers and senior government officials ever held, the Preparatory Commission on World Food Proposals, sat from October 1946 to January 1947. Its conclusions and recommendations were that:

1. these objectives could be achieved only in an expanding world economy;
2. they required the industrialization and agricultural development of the under-developed countries;
3. this in turn required finance, mostly from national sources but the International Bank should play a more active role;

4. price stabilization should be sought through intergovernmental commodity agreements, using buffer stocks, famine reserves and sometimes export quotas as occasion might require;
5. exporting countries should arrange special-price sales of surplus commodities for nutrition schemes in importing countries;
6. pending the establishment of an International Trade Organization, an Interim Co-ordinating Committee for International Commodity Arrangements should be established in conjunction with the Economic and Social Council;
7. the Annual Session of the FAO Conference hold a review and consultation as to production and nutrition programmes; and finally
8. a Council of FAO or "World Food Council" be set up to act between sessions of the Conference.

When these comprehensive proposals came before the Third (Geneva) Session of the FAO Conference they were "approved and implemented," which in practice meant doing little about the first five recommendations, adopting the annual programme review as a regular feature on the Conference agenda and establishing the Council of FAO, composed of 18 governments (later increased to 24) in place of the then existing Executive Committee composed of outstanding individuals not representative of governments. This was felt generally by governments to be a satisfactory and expeditious way of disposing of an awkward changeling.

It was a far cry from the World Food Board idea of three large international funds for buffer stocks, famine reserve and surplus disposal, respectively; and, as for large-scale credits for development, it was to be another eight years before this idea could be seriously entertained.

However, the creation of the Council of FAO and the institution of the annual programme review greatly strengthened the international machinery for watching movements in production or trade and, to service these meetings, the FAO Secretariat started its useful publication *The State of Food and Agriculture*.

Thus ended Sir John's grand design. As a practical proposal it was a non-starter. As a platform for ventilating the heartfelt ideas of many governments, mainly the smaller and poorer ones, it was invaluable. And the issues it raised and faced still come up year after year at one meeting or another and will so continue until in prosperity or crisis the groping nations find some acceptable solutions.

Before the matter was laid to rest, there was one attempt at a comeback. The FAO Council Session, held in Paris in June 1949, requested the Director-General (by then Norris E. Dodd) to report on "the underlying causes of emerging commodity trade problems together with recommendations for possible action by governments." As usual with international resolutions, the Council expected to get his report in the impossibly short time of four months. An advisory body of experts, with John B. Condliffe of the University of California as chairman, had to be assembled and had to work in a hurry, when, after previous experiences, what was wanted was a most sober and careful appraisal of the subject. They diagnosed the immediate problem as an accumulation of surpluses in hard currency countries — principally the dollar area — while countries with weak inconvertible currencies were still finding it difficult to import sufficient for their needs. Their recommendations included the establishment of an International Commodity Clearing House (ICCH) whose functions would be:

1. to move food from surplus to deficit countries by accumulating payment in inconvertible currencies to the credit of the selling countries until general convertibility could be restored;
2. to organize and supervise sale at concessional prices of surpluses that still existed after the above;
3. after general convertibility had been achieved, to hold and operate buffer stocks.

These proposals, in their different style, were no nearer to being found practicable by most governments than those of Sir John Boyd Orr. The proposals failed to appreciate sufficiently the damage to financial confidence which would be caused by knowledge of the quantities of inconvertible currencies accumulating in the hands of ICCH. They ignored the difficulty that these blocked balances were incompatible with the idea of a revolving fund. They also gave inadequate attention to the intricate problems of trying to ensure that any surpluses disposed of at concessional prices would be additional to and not in substitution for the volume of the same products which would otherwise move through normal trade channels at normal market prices.

The 1949 Session of the FAO Conference rejected these proposals outright. As to surpluses arising through currency difficulties, the Conference confessed that it saw no remedy; as to those arising from other causes, it recommended that more vigorous use be made of the Interim Co-ordinating Committee for International Commodity Arrangements (ICCICA) — an institutional remnant from the discarded scaffolding of the International Trade Organization (ITO).

However, the Conference established, under the Council, a Committee on Commodity Problems (CCP), composed of 14 Member Governments to advise on the agricultural surplus commodity situation arising out of balance-of-payment difficulties. Its functions were:

1. to consider statements of needs received from governments experiencing difficulties in getting supplies and transmit them to governments with surpluses;
2. to consider proposals from governments with surpluses for disposing of these on special terms;
3. to review information generally and, where considered desirable, to initiate international action.

A year later the restriction to balance-of-payment problems in the Committee's terms of reference was removed and it was empowered to review all commodity problems.

This Committee, which is still in existence and which in 1953 had its membership increased to 20, has proved its worth as a forum for further examination of some of the many issues in this highly complex field. Because the trade questions with which it deals are tightly controlled these days by governments, it is vital that discussion should be conducted primarily by accredited government representatives who can say what policies are and what are not possible for their governments to contemplate. The FAO Secretariat has, for its part, contributed by carefully segregating different parts of the field for discussion and by analysing individual questions, as for instance the components of the various types of intergovernmental commodity arrangements. The Committee issued comparatively few reports in its early years.

In 1952, on the request of the FAO Conference, it examined the feasibility of establishing an emergency food reserve to be available promptly to countries threatened with famine. It suggested three possibilities:

1. a stock of food owned by an international agency;
2. a central fund administered by an international agency for purchasing and distributing food;
3. emergency food stocks held by national governments for international use.

Subsequently, a panel of five government experts expressed preference for the second suggestion, but the 1953 Conference of FAO did not favour taking further action at that time. More recently the CCP has devoted attention to surplus disposal problems which have again become topical in 1954 and 1955, especially because the United States Government has sought to export on special terms part of the large stocks of agricultural commodities which it holds. The CCP set up a working party in Washington which approved, after much deliberation, a set of principles that found acceptance by the CCP and later by the FAO Council. They sought to define matters which governments engaged in surplus disposal programmes should attend to in order to ensure that the programme should cause no harmful interference with normal patterns of production and international trade.[1] The FAO Council suggested that Member Governments be invited formally to adhere to this statement of principles and the majority have done so. (This, incidentally, may represent a useful new technique of securing acceptance of a code of behaviour, being much less cumbersome than formal ratification by governments.)

Meantime, the CCP substantially enlarged the working party into a standing sub-committee in Washington, which in turn has working parties on individual commodities likely to be included in disposal programmes. This affords convenient machinery for governments to make known their anxieties and difficulties *before* any surpluses are actually moved. Although *ad hoc* at present, the arrangement bears striking analogy in reverse to the IEFC, albeit in microcosm.

Looking back over the past decade it is difficult to evaluate fairly what governments have been able to achieve through FAO, or otherwise, in the handling of shortages and surpluses. History never exactly repeats itself and, although the post-war period has indeed been characterized first by shortages and later by surpluses as everyone prophecied, the timing of these phases turned out different from the general expectation. The period of shortages lasted much longer than most people anticipated while the

---

[1] *Disposal of Agricultural Surpluses*, FAO Commodity Policy Study, No. 5, June 1954.

advent of surpluses was also much delayed, partly by the Korean war. Moreover, when surpluses did develop they were not world-wide and catastrophic, forcing governments into radical action; they were local and particular, affecting certain countries and certain commodities only. On the other hand, fluctuations in prices of some primary products have been as violent over the past decade as at any time in the inter-war period.

As to methods for dealing with surpluses, the Geneva reformers had envisaged that they would be absorbed through a world-wide rise in nutritional levels, while Hot Springs added the further panacea of commodity agreements. During the last ten years many countries have become to a considerable degree nutrition conscious and many governments have developed programmes of special food distribution to vulnerable groups. These have not, however, been on such a scale as to form effective channels for the disposal of most surplus foods, and it is unlikely that they could ever fulfil this function. There is, however, one exception. The surplus of skimmed milk powder has been used to a large extent in feeding children. Millions of children in all parts of the world have benefited from the glut of processed milk in great dairying countries, notably the United States. The wide-scale distribution of dried skimmed milk through the United Nations Children's Fund (UNICEF) is among the important and striking results of the new trends in thought and action described in this book.

The other panacea, commodity agreements, has proved disappointing. Governments have concluded only two agreements for food-stuffs — wheat and sugar — and except possibly for olive oil there is no immediate sign of more. They debated for months at London, Geneva and Havana the principles of commodity policy and the prospective responsibilities of the International Trade Organization, but that body never was born. Instead we have a CCP, an ICCICA, a new United Nations Commission for International Commodity Stabilization, and in the commercial field, the General Agreement on Tariffs and Trade (GATT).

The objective set before the Bruce Commission of " stabilizing prices at levels fair to producers and consumers alike" proved illusive; the world is not a step nearer, perhaps further off since some of the stabilizing factors, like long-term contracts, are being abandoned. The disturbing recommendations of Sir John Boyd Orr and of the ICCH experts involving large central financing found no favour at all.

Such a lean harvest over ten years should stimulate the question : what went wrong ? Were the Geneva and Hot Springs objectives misconceived? Have governments deliberately reneged on the policies they once professed ? Has the Secretariat failed to provide the services and/or the leadership ?

Probably all these questions can be honestly answered in the negative, for we confront here difficulties which lie deep in the structure of modern society. We face the dilemma described in Chapter II, namely that the institutions which peoples set up through their own governments to guide and control their economic destinies hinder and in many cases preclude in the short run at least the setting up of analogous institutions at the international level to guide and control international economic life. The economic readjustment tasks in the advanced countries and the development tasks in the under-developed countries have laid further burdens upon governments in their administration of economic policy. Furthermore, it is only quite recently that certain governments have developed machinery for regulating a variety of national problems — exchange control, import regulation, capital issue control, capital export licensing, price regulation, organization of marketing, government holding of strategic or surplus stocks, and so on — and in many cases the machinery is still experimental and on trial. Small wonder that, under these circumstances, most governments have been wary of undertaking international commitments which might limit their freedom of action in respect of commercial and commodity policy. And all this applies with particular force to agriculture, the most regulated of industries. Governments are so committed to protecting and supporting the incomes of their farm communities that they feel unable to participate in international arrangements which might require them to modify this protection and support.

The road to satisfactory international integration lies not through abolishing all national controls, as some thought in the 'thirties, but rather through co-ordinating the national controls in the general interest — a difficult road demanding much patience, for advances are scored in yards not miles.

Nevertheless, some advance has been achieved, especially since the CCP settled down to its unassuming work. Although superficially it would seem that the committee had laid down only negative criteria for action by governments, in fact it has, by detailed examination of the many components of the problems, enabled governments to adopt positive measures, should the need arise, either individually or in concert. This work will make it possible to limit the extent to which governments expose themselves to risks when they undertake certain forms of international commodity action; and it is only when the price which governments might have to pay has been brought down to an acceptable figure, so to speak, that their peoples will permit them to engage in international commitments of this kind.

During the past decade, apart from the shortages dealt with by IEFC, there has been no great compulsion to international action in the commodity field; no one country has been badly hurt yet. It is to be hoped that a substantial further period may elapse before governments are powerfully constrained to act, so that before then the preparatory work of the CCP and other bodies may be further advanced and the ground better prepared.

In all this the role of the FAO Secretariat has included keeping the topic alive throughout a most unpromising period, unostentatious spade-work in studying and clarifying the issues, and constantly seeking out new opportunities for bringing governments together to get something constructive done. This persistence is facilitating the evolution of an international code of behaviour in respect to commodity policy, and an acceptable and accepted code of behaviour represents a considerable advance on the law of the jungle.

Chapter VI

INTELLIGENCE SERVICE

Norris E. Dodd defined FAO's major responsibilities in two categories :[1]

1. maintaining an intelligence service for Member Governments and for its own staff to be utilized in the action programmes it operates;
2. framing and developing action programmes to supplement those initiated by governments and in which FAO, on the request of such governments, is in a position to participate.

One of FAO's active programmes, namely in the field of international economic policy, has been discussed in the previous chapter. The many other action programmes in the more technical fields will be considered in Chapter VII. What has been built up by way of an intelligence service is the subject of the present chapter.

In his same report the Director-General went on to say:

---

[1] *The Work of FAO 1952/53.* Introduction, p. 2.

Intelligence may be collected in many ways — from printed publications, from government replies to questionnaires, from meetings of expert consultants, from visits of FAO technicians to member countries. It is disseminated in year-books, monthly bulletins, abstracts, at meetings, in public announcements, by press, film, radio, in the briefing of experts and in servicing missions.

As this definition so rightly implies, no hard and fast line can be drawn between information and action; the one leads frequently into the other. Thus, for example, the FAO Secretariat may issue a report on the preparation of rinderpest vaccine or it may send a man to a country to explain orally and by demonstration how it is done. Again, a government may obtain through FAO a mission which surveys a certain problem and submits a report; alternatively, the government may ask for a team of experts to consult and advise. The first procedure adds a document to the "intelligence service," while the second is classed as "technical assistance." On the other hand, some FAO publications, such as statistical year-books and abstracts, contain no direct "action" element.

The Hot Springs Conference passed no resolution concerned specifically with the provision of an international intelligence service for food and agriculture, though the need for one was implied in many of the decisions which that Conference reached. At Quebec, by contrast, special attention was given to describing the sort of intelligence service governments expected to have provided. The Conference through Commission A set up a special committee on statistics which laid down the statistical requirements in respect of nutrition and food consumption, rural welfare, agricultural production, fisheries, forestry and forest products and marketing.

> It is a matter of the greatest urgency to resume as rapidly as possible the publication of international agricultural statistics and the series formerly collected and published by the International Institute of Agriculture, the *Centre international de sylviculture* and the *Comité international du bois.*

Likewise the committees working in the special subject fields of nutrition, agriculture, fisheries and forestry requested that the Secretariat should provide a wide range of technical publications on these subjects. To quote the report of the technical committee on agriculture:

> FAO should serve as an international clearing-house of technical and other information in the field of food and agriculture. In its publications it should include surveys of particular regional or world-wide problems and summaries of significant scientific developments. It also should assemble and make available world-wide summaries of legislative enactments and policies relating to food and agriculture. It should publish, or arrange for the publication of, annotated bibliographies and abstracts and make available on request microfilm and photostatic reproductions of important documents.

The FAO Secretariat should also maintain a roster of experts with particulars of their qualifications and experience; it should further the exchange of information by calling meetings of specialists, it should assist governments in the exchange of scientists, educators, students, etc., and should promote the establishment of specialized programmes for teaching and research. As already noted, the governments who conceived of FAO primarily as a recording agency had a lot to say at Quebec.

What has been done about these resolutions during the ten succeeding years? What services has the Secretariat brought into existence? How are they regarded? What additions, if any, are being requested? What changes, if any, in treatment and presentation? It will be convenient to treat of the intelligence service in three distinct sectors — statistical and economic; scientific and technical; abstracts, digests and library.

In providing statistical and economic intelligence the Secretariat was slow off the mark; little was produced during the first two years. In 1946, it is true, there appeared the *World Food Survey,* giving pre-war food consumption data for 70 countries, but while the analysis and presentation was undertaken by the Secretariat, the statistics were prepared by a panel of outsiders using techniques and materials worked out during the war, mainly in the United States and Britain for allocation and relief calculations.

For the next two years statistical work was virtually confined to the Secretariat of IEFC, which made its compilations available to governments in mimeographed form. This work covered production, import, export, domestic utilization and consumption statistics of the commodities under international allocation. The FAO Secretariat was trying to collect the same data through somewhat different channels and with limited success. It was not until the IEFC activity began to taper off in 1948 that the FAO services got under way, and only then began the regular periodic publication of the statistical year-books (agricultural production and trade, forestry, fisheries), monthly statistical bulletins, commodity bulletins and the annual report, *The State of Food and Agriculture*.

At Quebec a number of governments had assumed that FAO, in taking over and absorbing the International Institute of Agriculture, would take over as a going concern its section concerned with the collection and publication of statistics, and undoubtedly much time would have been saved and many mistakes would have been avoided had this been done. The Institute had long experience in the field and had over the years learned how to obtain data expeditiously from governments and get it quickly into print, a series of processes far from being as simple as they sound. Unfortunately the Institute and all its works was over-discredited as *ancien régime*; its know-how and staff were ignored while a new, largely Anglo-American staff sat in Washington learning the hard way. It took them a long time to acquire the techniques of collecting current information from governments and to master the procedures for orderly arrangement and timely publication. Rather late in the day, senior members of the IIA staff were consulted and a few were hired.

Another reason for delay was the so-called *Article XI Reports*, by which according to the FAO Constitution:

> Each Member Nation shall communicate periodically to the Organization reports on the progress made toward achieving the purpose of the Organization set forth in the Preamble and on the action taken on the basis of recommendations made and conventions submitted by the Conference...
> Each Member Nation shall, on request, communicate to the Organization, all laws and regulations and official reports and statistics concerning nutrition, food and agriculture.

It was at first planned to obtain all these various types of information in a single annual packet, from each government, but after two years' experiments this was found too cumbersome; statistics were taken out and made the subject of separate questionnaires for monthly and for annual series. Still later it was found that by arranging for regular receipt of national publications and by staff visits to countries, the Secretariat could keep itself more fully informed as to programmes and other developments in member countries than through the *Article XI Reports*.

In due course, however, the statistical service settled down and can now claim to cover Member Governments' requirements within the limits of its financial resources.

In one matter a very prompt beginning was made, namely in preparation for the 1950 World Census of Agriculture, as requested at the Quebec Conference. In order to influence the census arrangements of national governments, it was necessary to convene far in advance the various meetings of statistical experts at which a measure of agreement could be reached on definitions, categories and methodology. Energetic action in this field by the Secretariat resulted in the census being taken in no fewer than 102 countries and territories on bases which ensured a high degree of comparability in the data collected. The Secretariat has followed up this initiative by action to encourage and promote timely publication of the results. A prompt start was likewise made upon a world forest inventory.

The Secretariat also initiated in another field some work quite pioneering in character, namely the statistical measurement of the volume of agricultural production throughout the world. For this it also called in panels of outside experts to determine how to overcome the formidable methodological problems involved. In consequence, it is now possible to measure the agricultural output in value and volume terms in each country on a common basis, so that, approximate though the figures may be, progress can be compared as between countries and so that the individual figures can be agglomerated into an index of world agricultural production. This statistical tool proves useful in many directions; for example, it facilitates calculations and comparisons of output per worker, output per acre and output per farm.

On the economic side, the Secretariat, at the request of the Conference, particularly arising out of the recommendations of the Preparatory Committee on World Food Proposals, initiated a new service, namely "outlook reports," projections of what might happen to output, trade, prices and consumption over the next year or, in some cases, five years. This service supplemented the programme review undertaken at each session of the Conference and at regional economic meetings. If governments were to confer together as to desirable adjustments in their national programmes, it was no use merely having statistical data relating to the past. They needed "best informed guesses" as to what was going to happen in the period ahead. This service has often been misunderstood and hence criticized. It has not been designed, Joseph-like, as predictions of events to come; it claims no more than to evaluate, sometimes statistically, sometimes not, the factors influencing a given market or situation, so that trends can be discerned or opposing tendencies weighed. This service becomes especially valuable at the present time when governments in many countries face the problems of selective expansion, of encouraging some production lines and discouraging others.

In the fields of fisheries and of forestry and forest products, similar outlook studies have been prepared and meetings held. In fisheries there have been studies and meetings on the production and market outlook for herring and also for whitefish. The *European Timber Trends and Prospects* study was, methodologically, a pioneer among commodity studies, and the conclusions drawn from its analysis of longer-term prospects were of great import to foresters, forest industries and consumers. More recently, a survey of *World Pulp and Paper Resources and Prospects* has focussed attention on paper shortages as a brake on educational and cultural advance in the less developed countries, and has stimulated an action programme to redress the situation.

Turning now to the technical and scientific intelligence service provided by the Organization, the range of subject matter is so large and the type of material selected for publication so various that no concise picture of the whole can be given. The reader is asked to turn to the appendix where he will find grouped by subjects a listing of the principal papers, studies and reports which come under this heading. In addition to the publications listed, there is a large quantity of mimeographed material in the shape of reports of technical meetings, papers prepared for the FAO Council and Conference, documents submitted to other agencies or to joint bodies between FAO and other agencies.

Though the lists are long and impressive, it is at once apparent that as yet they cover only parts of their respective fields. In many cases the reasons for the choice so far made are obvious; for example, the mammoth work on the *World Catalogues of Genetic Stocks* has had to be confined so far to the two crops most important to the peoples of the world; namely, wheat and rice. Likewise the nutritional studies, *Rice and Rice Diets* and *Maize and Maize Diets* were undertaken because these are the most typical and widespread diets of the malnourished people of the world. Sometimes publications are prepared in response to urgent requests from a number of governments; for instance, *Rinderpest Vaccines* and *Zebu Cattle of India and Pakistan*, or *Fish Farming and Inland Fishery Management in Rural Economy*. Some may originate from an initiative taken and resolution adopted in another agency; thus it was a resolution of the Economic and Social Council in 1950 which stimulated the FAO studies, *Land Reform, Communal Land Tenure* and the *Inter-relationship between Agrarian Reform and Agricultural Development*. Some publications report the results of some international collaborative effort, such as *Cooperative Hybrid Maize Tests in European and Mediterranean Countries*.

In some cases the publications succeed each other according to a conscious plan; the treatment of soils problems provides an example of this. The starting point was the documentation needs of the Fertilizer Committee of the IEFC, for which a world survey of fertilizer consumption requirements and production availabilities was prepared. This was followed by *World Fertilizer Pro-*

duction and Consumption and Targets for the Future. In a number of countries fertilizers were beginning to be used on a substantial scale for the first time and the desire was expressed for some guidance from FAO as to their most efficient use. The Secretariat, having sought advice as to the best procedure from a small panel, enlisted the co-operation of 36 specialists from some 14 countries in preparing a monograph: *Efficient Use of Fertilizers* of which some 15,000 copies in three languages have been sold or distributed. Next, the International Rice Commission set up a Working Party on Fertilizers which has circulated progress reports and pursuant to its recommendations, training centres on Soil Fertility Practices have been held at Coimbatore and at Himayatsagar, India. In 1951 a Latin American meeting on Fertilizer Production, Distribution and Utilization was held; subsequently, a *Soil Erosion Survey of Latin America* was published, following a previous more general survey entitled *Soil Conservation: An International Study*. The desire to use fertilizers and soils more efficiently especially in underdeveloped countries, led to an interest in the techniques of soil survey; so, in 1953, a monograph, *Soil Surveys for Land Development* was published. This in turn led to consideration of the problems of soil classification and a meeting of soil scientists was arranged to discuss first the European aspects of this. For this work to progress there must be some international understanding as to definitions and nomenclature; accordingly FAO set about preparing the *Multilingual Vocabulary of Soil Science* which was finally published in 1954 in eight languages.

This concentrated summary of the intelligence service provided in one single field illustrates not only the conscious planning of the programme of publications and meetings but also how one activity breeds another and branches out in new directions.

Examination of FAO publications reveals wide differences in mode of treatment — some reports presented in quasi-popular style, others in highly technical language. In each case an attempt is made to gauge the type of public that will be interested in the topic under discussion and to adapt the treatment to the readers. This objective, admirable in theory, presents difficulties in application. A scientific worker in Afghanistan is not the same as a scientific worker in Denmark, nor does the director of a statistical office in say Cambodia have the same interests as his counterpart in Canada. Compromises have to be made and as such may cause dissatisfaction in certain quarters. On the whole, however, the bulk of the more technical publications is addressed to the people — scientists and administrators — of the under-developed countries, and this is the more true since the technical assistance activity has come to assume such importance.

It should be pointed out here that publications are by no means the only vehicle that FAO uses for disseminating technical information. Meetings and working parties are an important medium. Examples of the many held each year are the Working Party on Mediterranean Pasture and Fodder Development, the Caribbean Agricultural Extension Development Centre, the Asia and Far East Centre on Land Problems, the Near East Meeting on Irrigation and Drainage. At such meetings technicians and administrators from developed and from under-developed countries are able to exchange their knowledge and experience. It is, of course, difficult to say when meetings of this kind have primarily the character of disseminating information and when the character of technical assistance; there neither is, nor need be, any hard and fast line.

The last of the three parts of the intelligence service includes abstracts, bibliographies, digests, periodicals, library and information service. In regard to abstracting services there was much discussion at the birth of FAO as to how much the Organization should attempt in this field. Any abstracting service is comparatively expensive in men and money if it is to provide world coverage and, moreover, such services already existed in one country or another for many sectors of the field. The view prevailed that FAO should encourage existing abstracting services to extend and improve their coverage and should itself enter the field only in sectors where it proved impossible to get the job done by some other body. In the event, only in fisheries has FAO undertaken the task, and *World Fisheries Abstracts* appears bi-monthly. (The Forestry Division has issued a volume, *Forestry Abstracts Coverage List*, prepared for it by the British Commonwealth Forestry Bureau.)

Bibliography is also a field in which the FAO Secretariat prefers to leave projects to other bodies, but it has published some, including: a *Bibliography of Forestry and Forest Products*, one on *Land Tenure*, one on *Fishing Gear and Methods*, and, akin to bibliographies, also directories: a *World Directory of Manufacturers and Suppliers of Equipment for the Fishing Industry, a *Directory of Forestry Schools*, and a *Directory of Wheel and Crawler Tractors Produced Throughout the World*.

As to digests, there was a long-established service of the IIA covering Agricultural Legislation and, to meet a desire of Member Governments, this service has been resumed and extended to include some aspects of food and nutrition; *Food and Agricultural Legislation* is published quarterly.

In certain fields the technical periodical or bulletin has been found an appropriate means of spreading information and of keeping in touch with technical workers in that subject around the world. Thus the quarterly *Unasylva* offers a review of all matters relating to forestry and forest products. The quarterly *FAO Fisheries Bulletin* performs a similar service in its sphere, though somewhat more technical in content. Still more technical, the *FAO Plant Protection Bulletin* (monthly) provides a service specified for in the International Plant Protection Convention of 1951. It should be added that the *Monthly Bulletin of Agricultural Economics and Statistics* carries, as its name suggests, articles on a variety of economic questions as well as its regular statistical tables.

As a service to students from all over the world as well as for its staff, FAO maintains at Rome its own library, now aptly christened "The David Lubin Memorial Library." This combines the library of the former IIA, the collection which FAO assembled in Washington prior to its move to Rome, and lastly the Geneva Forestry Library. This joint collection, to which FAO regularly adds, constitutes something unique in scope and completeness. It is doubtful if any other subject field is so well provided internationally in this respect as food and agriculture.

Finally, FAO maintains an information service to provide data as to its activities to public and private bodies and associations of all kinds. It supplies material for newspaper articles, radio scripts, films, lectures, exhibitions and the like. It keeps in touch with the national farm organizations and other non-governmental bodies with which FAO has contacts. It provides visual materials for training centres and materials for lectures at schools and colleges. Much of its work is decentralized through regional information offices, so as to be in closer touch with the publicity and educational services of individual countries.

This then is the record of ten years' work in publication and dissemination of knowledge. It is a rather costly task to keep this service going at a high level of quality and punctuality. In 1954 the expenditure on "documents" was 760,000 dollars out of a total expenditure of 5,500,000 dollars, or about 14 percent. This covered editing, typing, translating, printing or mimeographing and distribution of publications proper, and the about equal volume of working papers arising from Conference, Council and other bodies. It charged nothing for the salaries of members of the technical staff involved in authorship. It costs money to give out all the principal publications and working papers in three languages, but it will cost even more if China and the U.S.S.R. join the Organization and their languages have to be used too.

The service has to be the result of a compromise. Government delegations to the Conference invariably ask for a variety of different and often conflicting publications; they cannot all be satisfied. While the statistical and economic intelligence service finds as good a reception in the developed as in the under-developed countries, the technical publications are oriented primarily to the needs of the latter, it being assumed, probably rightly, that the advanced countries have their own arrangements for keeping abreast of current developments in the diverse scientific and technical fields.

It has taken a long time in respect to statistical publications to regain the standard formerly set by the IIA and, compared therewith, perhaps FAO still has something to learn as to manner of presentation for the convenience of the using public.

In scientific and technical subjects it took a while to emancipate the monographs from an undue preponderance of United States examples and sources, but now the extent and the standard of what is issued goes far beyond the achievements of the IIA, as indeed might be expected, seeing the far greater staff and finance now available.

By way of postscript, it should be explained that, although many of FAO's publications have significant technical assistance content and value, virtually none of them are financed from the funds of the Expanded Technical Assistance Programme; they are carried on the budget of the regular programme.

Chapter VII

TECHNICAL ACTIVITIES

Were the object of this book to catalogue in all its details the whole of the technical work of the FAO Secretariat and of governments working through FAO, then it would be a much longer document and at this point there should rightly come a series of chapters recounting the growth of intergovernmental and secretariat activity in each of the subject fields. There would be a chapter on land reform so fundamental to all other agricultural improvements, one on home economics and nutritional education, one on fisheries' resource conservation, one on forest management, one on extension and advisory services. There might be 15 or 20 such chapters.

But this book is concerned not so much with the activities of FAO, as with how these activities were moulded into shape by ideas and events, and since there was really one clear train of thinking which led to this technical work and all its manifestations, it seems reasonable to compress into one chapter the story of how governments came to use FAO in the technical fields and to leave for another publication a comprehensive account of the programmes themselves. One or two individual programmes will be mentioned as examples but no attempt is made here to offer a representative account of all that is going on.

The idea that FAO should be used for passing on scientific knowledge and technical procedures was not born in 1949 when the technical assistance concept first came into general public discussion; it dates back to the beginnings of the Organization. Thus at Hot Springs:

> The natural sciences are a particularly fruitful field for international collaboration because they are themselves international; basic physical and biological laws are the same everywhere and are universally accepted. There is already a good deal of collaborating but much more could be done. Joint planning and exchange of information services, materials and personnel could and should be carried out in such a way that nations would be encouraged and assisted in enlarging agricultural research applicable to their problems while costly duplication would be reduced.[1]

This represented only a vague groping toward the new idea; the resolutions mostly referred to what nations should do at home, not what they should do through FAO.

However, the function was specifically mentioned in the Constitution of FAO. Article I, paragraph 3 (a) reads : " It shall also be the function of the Organization to furnish such technical assistance as governments may request."

The Quebec Conference produced a very different climate of opinion. The particular faith of the people and government of the United States that agriculture could be revolutionized within perhaps a generation by the application of science found full expression and strong support.

---

[1] *Report of the Conference*, Section II.

Fortified by the preparatory work in this matter of the Interim Commission [2] the delegations at Quebec spelled out at length and in detail the character of the technical services which FAO should render to their peoples. Thus in the report of Commission A (Introduction):

> In agriculture as in nutrition some of the most urgent problems are in the less developed countries, especially the densely populated ones. FAO can serve the immediate needs of these countries with information on seeds, fertilizers, pesticides, machines and hand tools, and with help in developing extension services to advise farmers and demonstrate better methods. Equally important but taking longer to develop are programmes for soil improvement — so essential to feeding the rapidly increasing population of the earth — irrigation, livestock and crop improvement, credit and cooperation.

This statement, as well as the reports of the committees which it summarized, has significance from several angles. It shows governments already at that date expecting FAO to provide technical assistance over a wide range of subjects; it directs this assistance specifically toward the less developed countries, and it links the whole endeavour not to the then acute world food shortages but to the " rapidly increasing population of the earth. " It gives clear and concrete expression to the ideas which, after more ferment in men's minds, were to emerge four years later as " Point IV. "

The Director-General himself also saw what programmes would be needed to enable all people to have diets " on a health standard. " In FAO's first major publica-

---

[2] *The Work of FAO.* United Nations Interim Commission on Food and Agriculture (Washington, D. C., August 1945).

tion, the *World Food Survey*, there appears such a comprehensive account of what he called " the heart of the problem, " including industrial as well as agricultural development, that it seems worth reproducing in full:

> The heart of the problem is to increase individual productivity..... The output of food is ten times greater in the advanced than in the poorer countries. The conclusion is inescapable that food for the world can be produced in much greater abundance by fewer hands.
>
> Land resources everywhere are limited. When population presses too heavily on these resources rural under-employment and inefficiency are inevitable. Human abilities stagnate during a good part of the year. Able-bodied men and women produce only a pittance by their labour. The whole year's work on many a farm in the under-developed countries could be done in a few days by one man with modern equipment and practices.
>
> The way out of this situation is to open up resources other than those of farming for the bulk of the population. The opportunities for the use of human skill, through the application of modern science and technology, in the production of goods and services other than food are enormous. By developing them, opportunities will at the same time be opened for those remaining on the land to increase their efficiency manyfold.
>
> This calls for rapid, large-scale development of industry and trade, and of educational and other services. For that purpose, large investment both of capital and of technical skill will be needed. The only alternative to this investment for the western world is to restrict its own high production. The investment will be profitable because it will vastly increase the productivity and the purchasing power of millions of human beings. The improvement of agriculture in the less developed countries will in itself result in large demands for tools, machinery, fertilizers, transportation equipment, processing equipment, and other material, as well as for consumer goods to meet the needs of more prosperous farm populations.

Such advances for great populations and areas of the globe can occur only if the problem is considered a world problem and the challenge a world challenge. The poorer countries cannot master the problem or meet the challenge alone, especially in the present state of development of their material and human resources. All nations will gain by world advances in human health and well-being and in production and trade, and all must participate in bringing them to pass.

Many people who have given serious study to the population problem prophecy doom for much of mankind unless the rate of population growth can be drastically checked. It is worth reiterating that the fundamental solution to the problem lies in increasing the productivity of the individual by putting at his disposal modern scientific knowledge and the tools of modern technology. To the extent that this is done, every individual can become a source of new wealth to his country and to the world. To the extent that it is not done, he is a potential liability, unable to supply his own needs, let alone helping to supply those of his fellow human beings.

To put this knowledge and these tools at the disposal of millions of human beings who have never had them requires vision and boldness in the best sense and the highest degree. It must be emphasized that half-way measures will not do. If they are the best that can be devised, the situation will become more and more hopeless, and the prophecies of doom will come to pass. A little amelioration here, a half-hearted attempt at improvement there will serve in the future, as it has in the past, only to increase the numbers of the poverty-stricken and ignorant. The difficulties in the way of formulating and putting into effect vigorous concerted measures for industrial and agricultural development that will open up new opportunities for these people are very great, but they must be solved or the world faces a future of universally lower living standards or of wars and revolutions that will force the issue.

In this passage can be found adumbrated a great deal of what was to come; assumption by the advanced nations of responsibility for helping the under-developed countries with finance and techniques, emphasis on industrial equally with agricultural development, the profitability of investment in development through generating increased demand the world over for goods and services, the size of the job and the vital necessity of speed if production is to win the race against population.

It is true that for the remainder of his period of office Sir John Boyd Orr devoted most of his energies to what appeared to be quite other matters — economic and financial. (He would have said that a World Food Board and a credit agency were prerequisites to technical assistance.) Nonetheless he saw to it that technical activities were built into the structure of FAO from the outset. Despite his preoccupations he found time in 1946 to organize a Mission to Greece followed by one to Poland and another to Siam. These missions studied, not the short-term rehabilitation needs, but the longer-term development requirements and laid foundations for technical assistance programmes. By way of follow-up in Greece, the Director-General sent a nutrition worker, who spent two years establishing nutrition programmes throughout the country.

Work was also initiated on grain storage, which led to technical assistance to Latin American countries to improve their storage facilities and reduce their losses of grain. The *World Catalogues of Wheat and Rice Genetic Stocks* were started.

By the beginning of 1947 it became apparent that UNRRA would soon be coming to an end and would, unless arrangements were made, be leaving considerable unfinished business in its rehabilitation programmes. Under an agreement concluded in February 1947, UNRRA turned over to FAO its outstanding rehabilitation programmes in agriculture together with the associated field staff and a sum of 1,135,000 dollars to complete the jobs. These programmes were located in European countries plus China, the Philippines and Ethiopia. It soon appeared unrealistic and impracticable to draw too severe a distinction in these programmes between rehabilitation and development — the one must lead into and prepare for the other. Thus, this batch of field workers could fairly be regarded in retrospect as the first contingent of FAO's technical assistance army.

Meanwhile, the Director-General was organizing other forms of help. A nutritionist visited a number of countries to advise on dietary survey techniques; another to advise on the use of dried milk in school feeding programmes. To make a beginning on the central problem of South-east Asia — rice — an intergovernmental Rice Study Group was established, which later became the International Rice Commission and set up rice breeding and fertilizer working parties; both of these have become focal points for technical aid in the region.

By August 1948, *The Work of FAO* (the annual volume summarizing the year's work for the Conference) carried a chapter headed: "Technical Assistance and Special Projects," this being six months before President Truman's Point Four speech and a year before the United Nations agencies became seized with the idea. The chapter included accounts of technical meetings organized to facilitate the interchange of information between scientists who had not had opportunity to meet one another since before the war, fellowships granted with ex-UNRRA funds for the training of technical workers and distribution of materials for trials (e. g. seeds and vaccines), and of technical publications to institutions which had been cut off during the war from scientific contacts. The Director-General was able to report that specialists were already at work in ten countries covering such subjects as plant breeding, veterinary science, food refrigeration, entomology, irrigation, sylviculture, agricultural census, home economics, nutrition, farm machinery, fertilizer use, dairy industry, fisheries and extension services.

Previously, the 1947 Session of the Conference had asked FAO to assist governments to secure the services of qualified statistical experts and to arrange regional training facilities for census statisticians. It also recommended Member Governments to ask for nutrition experts. The 1948 Session of the Conference on receiving the Director-General's report referred to above, held a considerable debate on technical assistance procedures — the first of many — in which it agreed on a number of principles including (a) that experts must be really highly qualified people in their field; (b) that, before requesting experts, a government must have a definite programme with which the expert would be associated; and (c) that the expert should be chosen with special attention to the particular conditions and needs of the country. This may be reckoned a modest beginning in drawing up a code of behaviour acceptable in administering the assistance programme which has grown up swiftly during the last five years. The 1948 Session also asked the Secretariat to assist governments in the preparation of food balance sheets and in the orientation of their plans and programmes. It requested that a nutrition training course be held in the Near East.

A year or so later, FAO collaborated with WHO, in establishing a Standing Joint FAO/WHO Expert Committee on Nutrition which continues to give useful advice on problems common to both organizations.

By 1949 technical activities had grown to occupy two-thirds of the Director-General's Report to the Conference (*The Work of FAO*) and, looking to the future, he presented a draft of a two-year technical assistance programme. At this point FAO was feeling the financial strain. Requests for help were proliferating so fast that it was impossible to meet even all the most worthy ones and at the same time build up the intelligence services which governments also demanded; the budget would not allow it.

FAO had been the first of the new specialized agencies to be established. The Organization's budget was set at 5,000,000 dollars per annum in 1945 at a time when the inflationary tendencies and rising costs of the postwar period could not have been foreseen to an appreciable extent. In 1949 FAO's income bought much less than it did in 1945. If at this juncture new funds had not become available, someone would have had to invent them.

Before we pass on to discuss the emergence of a technical assistance programme in the United Nations and the specialized agencies it is perhaps worth pausing to clear up some confusion in language. The phrase "technical assistance," which in the early days of FAO was often used to describe all the technical activities, has since 1950 been confined more narrowly to mean the technical work of a special character financed under the ETAP programme including in its scope the sending of experts and limited supplies of equipment to countries, the organizing of training centres and the provision of fellowships (*see* below). And while this aspect of FAO's technical work has grown rapidly in volume and importance during the last five years the other aspects have also continued to develop and cater for vital needs. They include for example all work done in the agricultural, forestry, fishery, economic and nutritional fields in bringing governments together for joint action or for the formulation of common policies, technical meetings of experts to exchange information and to plan new lines of experimental work, the preparation and publication of technical studies and reports.

Of the great variety of technical activities which the Secretariat undertakes as part of its regular programme, as distinct from the ETAP programme, it may be useful to give just two examples, namely the International Plant Protection Convention and the work on foot-and-mouth disease in Europe.

The successful development of the International Plant Protection Convention illustrates a type of FAO activity which has far-reaching significance. The Convention was approved by the FAO Conference at its Sixth Session in 1951 and has since then been signed by 37 governments and adhered to by a number of others. The Convention has as its aim the promotion of international co-operation for combatting dangerous plant pests and diseases and restricting their spread to other countries. To this end, the governments which are parties to the Convention agree to set up national plant protection services which are staffed and equipped sufficiently to implement the terms of the Convention. Since plant pests and diseases are spread over long distances usually through infested plant materials, the Convention establishes uniform procedures for regulating the importation of plants to prevent invasions and, at the same time, to facilitate international trade. These procedures are now being followed closely by many countries. The Convention also provides for the organization of a world reporting service by FAO to circulate regularly information on the incidence of important pests and diseases in countries throughout the world. This service has been in operation for nearly three years and its usefulness has been widely recognized.

A second illustration is provided by European livestock production which over the past 50 years has repeatedly been affected by large-scale outbreaks of foot-and-mouth disease. These epizootics have flared up at intervals of five to seven years, gradually being eradicated or suppressed to endemic proportions in the intervening years.

The International Office of Epizootics (IOE) in Paris attempted to secure the information on these outbreaks and in turn warn neighbouring countries of the danger of spread of the disease. Despite this, large and widespread outbreaks continued to take their toll of European livestock and culminated in 1951 when outbreaks occurred in every European country except Ireland.

In this atmosphere, European governments were searching for some form of inter-country machinery which would ensure prompt reporting of outbreaks, make available information on the availability of stocks of virus and vaccine, co-ordinate research on standardization of diagnosis and better methods of control, initiate training centres for research workers in this field, and if an absolute emergency arose, help any country to suppress a large-scale epizootic.

Several preliminary meetings were held and in July 1953 the Director-General of FAO convened a meeting of a special Committee on Foot-and-Mouth Disease which met in Rome and was attended by representatives from many European countries. Arising out of the work of this Committee, the European Commission for the Control of Foot-and-Mouth Disease was established and in July 1954 held its first meeting which was attended by delegates from the six foundation member countries, as well as observers from eleven other European countries from IOE, OEEC, ECA and FAO.

Since that date three other countries have joined the Commission, which is giving practical effect to its terms of reference, namely, to improve reporting of the disease throughout Europe, list available stocks of virus and vaccine, and inaugurate research training centres.

It should also be mentioned that the activities of the three Regional Fisheries Councils and the four Regional Forestry Commissions likewise represent work being carried out under the regular programme of FAO.

To return to the history of "technical assistance" in its narrower connotation, the cumulative pressure of ideas found dramatic expression in President Truman's Point Four speech. He said:

> The grinding poverty and the lack of economic opportunity for many millions of people in the economically underdeveloped parts of Africa, the Near and Far East, and certain

regions of Central and South America, constitute one of the greatest challenges of the world today.....

The major effort in such a programme must be local in character, it must be made by the people of the underdeveloped areas themselves. It is essential, however, to the success of their effort that there be help from abroad. In some cases, the peoples of these areas will be unable to begin their part of this great enterprise without initial aid from other countries.

The story has been told elsewhere how, following President Truman's speech, the United States delegate to the United Nations proposed a technical assistance fund to which his government would contribute on a substantial scale if other governments would also give their share; how a working party representing the United Nations and the specialized agencies prepared a blueprint of the programme, the fund and the machinery required to administer it. With minor modifications this plan was accepted.

What was awkwardly called the "Expanded Technical Assistance Programme" (ETAP) was now launched. Contributions began to flow in during 1950. Of the planned United Nations Technical Assistance Fund of 20 million dollars, 13.3 million dollars was allocated out to the agencies by ECOSOC, and FAO was awarded 29 percent of this amount, or something over 5,000,000 dollars. Thus overnight the financial resources of FAO were doubled and the commitments already made to send more experts to member countries could be honoured.

Although requests for aid snowballed, it was not prudent or practicable suddenly to start spending the full amount of the new funds. FAO desired to maintain the highest standards in the experts it recruited, in the briefing it gave them and in servicing the needs of countries; accordingly, the new field service had to be built gradually. FAO expenditure of ETAP funds has grown as follows:

1951	$ 2.0 million
1952	$ 6.2 "
1953	$ 5.9 "
1954	$ 4.7 "

In 1955 the expenditure is expected to exceed 7.7 million dollars. In addition, of course, some part of the so-called regular programme funds finance projects which are of technical assistance character.

This is a picture of accelerating progress and it would go on thus if FAO were not by now (1955) spending to the limit of its ETAP funds. When an expert works at his job in a country, he cannot help seeing, and may be he calls government attention to other problems and other needs. In due time there come out of this requests for more experts or more fellowships. A regional training centre on one topic creates a demand for another on perhaps a different aspect of the same topic. In the situation as it is today, partly through shortage of suitable experts and partly for lack of funds, FAO turns down a great number of requests. Unfortunately, the United Nations Fund, as its title suggests, is expanded not " expanding, " and as yet at least governments are not willing to augment appreciably the flow of internationally provided aid or to give the long-term assurance of continuing support which is essential to the effective achievement of its objective.

By the end of 1951 FAO had already recruited 322 experts and was servicing 56 countries or territories. Of these, 174 were still in the field. By mid-1953 there were 334 in the field and by mid-1955 over 400. The " export " and " import " of technical experts is by no means exclusively from advanced to under-developed countries; it is a movement in all directions. At the time of writing a Yugoslav statistician is working in Indonesia, a Pakistani in Liberia, an Indian soil technologist in Iran and a survey assistant from Jordan is working on irrigation schemes in Saudi Arabia. Through this programme the under-developed countries are not only helped to help themselves, but they are furnished opportunities to help each other. It is truly international, truly co-operative.

But, if under-developed countries are soon to help themselves, then their urgent need is to have a large number of their nationals trained in modern techniques, so that they in turn can become the advisers and leaders and demonstrators among their own people. To achieve this, governments have strongly demanded the provision of fellowships and the organization of training centres and FAO has been glad to meet the demand within the limits of its capacity.

As to fellowships, mostly for courses of study in developed countries, FAO by the end of 1951 had awarded 293, by mid-1953 this had risen to 469 and by the end of 1955 the number was expected to total 850. Countries making greatest use of this facility are Iran, Israel, Thailand, Yugoslavia, India and Syria. Nominations for fellowships often arise out of an expert's work. He will be looking round for someone to continue, after his departure, the work he has started, and he notices one or two men with the right aptitudes who, with training, would be competent to carry on the project. He approaches the government department concerned which, if it approves his suggestion, will seek to get this training item included in the government's next annual request to FAO. By these means it is usually possible to secure the award of fellowships to the men and women most likely to profit by them and to relate the subject-matter of the fellowships directly to the projects currently being developed in the country.

As to training centres, these may be organized either for a single country or for a group of countries and are located at some convenient point where equipment is available for the training in question. They may last a week or a month or on occasion longer, and the teachers and demonstrators will normally be an international team recruited by FAO. A great number of such centres have been and are being organized. (*See* Appendix II for illustrative list.) Yet what has been done is still but a drop in the ocean in relation to the immense needs of the under-developed countries for field workers, teachers, research workers and administrators.

The great bulk — 70 percent — of the expenditure under ETAP refers to individual projects to help individual countries, usually in the shape of small supplements to government enterprises, small, that is, in manpower and money but large and significant in effects. What happens in a particular case may be something like this.

* * *

Suppose that I am the Director of Agriculture of the Government of Country A. I am short of funds to carry out all the projects I might wish to, but more particularly I am short of trained staff, the few graduates in agricultural sciences having been assigned to key posts where they are already overburdened with work. The cotton crop, however, which provides a major portion of the country's income, is attacked by various pests and diseases which may be controlled if methods adopted in other countries are introduced. I have a small-scale plant protection programme in operation but I need expert advice in the best and most economical ways of tackling my plant protection problems and in helping to establish a field service for control work. I formulate a request for an expert adviser and I persuade my government to transmit it to FAO. Since there is already an FAO mission chief in my country I consult with him as to the kind of expert that would be of most use, and on the best way of explaining my problem and asking for assistance. With his help the request is sent in a precise and coherent form, in which it is more likely to be accepted by the technical staff in Rome.

The mission chief will, of course, ask what plans I have for following up and continuing the work after the expert leaves, and I have therefore prepared a continuation programme which means getting the finance minister to give me additional funds in his next budget. However, even with new funds I do not have the trained staff to carry on the continuation programme, so I ask the mission chief if he can arrange for two of my junior men to have a period of technical training in an institute or university overseas. These will work initially with the expert as his assistants, and even as interpreters, during the earlier part of his assignment; if they prove suitable and funds are available to FAO they are then granted fellowships. If FAO is unable to allocate fellowships in the current year, it is possible that a training centre is being organized within the region which my would-be Fellows could attend. Meanwhile, FAO submits the curriculum vitae of an expert for the approval of my government and with its concurrence the expert eventually arrives and stays in my country for six months. At first he seems perplexed by the (to him) strange surroundings, by the climate, soils and people, all of which are new to him. He says very little for the first week or so, but listens. Then gradually and surprisingly quickly he comes to grasp what our problems in plant production are. He begins to talk, to demonstrate and to advise. He outlines our immediate problems in pest control, tells us what chemicals and apparatus we need, and what the results of using these have been in other countries. He outlines our research needs and draws up a skeleton plan for an efficient field service. He points out the gaps in our technical staff and draws up a skeleton organization for a Plant Protection Division within the Ministry of Agriculture.

At the end of six months we are tremendously sorry to lose him and I think he too genuinely regrets leaving us. He leaves a report addressed through me to my government describing what he has accomplished and pointing out what remains to be done, with suggestions as to how to carry on. He had already discussed and agreed those suggestions with me and, of course, they entail modifications of the programme I had mapped out before he came. But I am sure these are for the best. After some tiresome delays, I get my additional vote, my two men return from their studies abroad or from a regional training centre and the work goes forward. About a year later a member of FAO Headquarters staff arrives to check on our progress and make sure we have not misunderstood or wasted the advice of the expert.

What does all this amount to? I am certain we have got this Plant Protection programme started years earlier than we would have in the absence of technical assistance. I know too that without that gentle outside pressure I would not have got that addition to my department's funds. Also without the fellowships or the training centre I would not have two men able to carry on the new work and to train others. I am now engaged on preparing another request in connection with the Animal Husbandry branch of my department.

* * *

Several hundred of these individual projects have been vividly described in Gove Hambidge's *The Story of FAO*. The majority of requests are related to agricultural production; on this sector some 60 percent of FAO's ETAP funds are spent. The remainder is divided among forestry, fisheries, nutrition, economic and statistical programmes. This distribution of effort reflects not only the overwhelming importance of agriculture in most countries' economies but also the great range of sciences and techniques involved in the management of soil, water, crops and livestock. The governments of the Near East have to date put in and had met more requests than those of any other region. On the other hand, Latin America obtains substantial technical aid direct from the United States outside of the United Nations programme, while in South-east Asia help is obtained under the Colombo Plan.

As mentioned earlier, FAO has found it expedient to organize part of its aid on a regional basis, for groups of countries. This saves men and money by bringing together people with common problems for joint action or study or training. Examples are the control measures, especially concerning pests and diseases, which can be taken effectively only by intergovernmental action. One example is the desert locust control centred round the Arabian peninsula in which since 1953 a dozen or more governments have co-operated under FAO auspices. Another is foot-and-mouth disease control for which FAO organized joint action in Central America and in Europe. Another is rinderpest control in Africa and South-east Asia. Yet another is irrigation where the waters to be used traverse two or more countries.

FAO has also found it convenient to conduct much of its technical work through regional bodies. These include:

> The European Committee on Agriculture
> European Commission for the Control of Foot-and-Mouth Disease
> Regional Committees under the Plant Protection Agreement
> Working Party on Desert Locust Control in the Near East
> General Fisheries Council for the Mediterranean
> Latin American Fisheries Commission (proposed)
> Asian Pacific Forestry Commission
> European Forestry Commission
> Near East Forestry Commission

TECHNICAL ACTIVITIES 127

> Latin American Forestry Commission
> International Rice Commission (although open to membership of any country is mainly concerned with South-east Asia).

Through these various bodies the people start helping themselves with FAO Secretariat acting as convener, consultant and recorder.

In addition to these permanent Organizations which meet periodically, special *ad hoc* meetings on a regional basis are held from time to time covering special fields, e. g.

> Mediterranean Pasture and Forestry Development
> European Extension and Vocational Training
> Olive Fly Control
> Handling of Timber in Mountainous Regions
> Livestock Improvement in Tropical and Subtropical Conditions
> European Land and Water Utilization and Conservation
> Forestry Production in the Far East
> Latin American Poplar Conference
> Forestry Development in Southern Europe
> Regional Meetings on Agricultual Production and Planning for the Far East, Near East, and Latin America, respectively.

There are also the many original training centres listed in Appendix III.

Another activity run on regional lines which deserves to be classed as technical assistance, although it is financed out of the regular budget of FAO, is the regional programme planning and outlook type of conference. These started in 1948 as " pre-Conference regional meetings " to conduct the component parts of the " programme review " called for by the Conference; they have developed into opportunities for administrative officials not merely to become acquainted with trends in other countries with a view to adjusting their own selective expansion programmes but also to learn more of the techniques of forward appraisal. Out of these meetings have come requests for training centres on programme planning, statistical sampling and seminars on agricultural development problems.

Beyond this there are co-operative projects between the ETAP and other agencies. Thus FAO joins with WHO in organizing nutrition courses, with ILO in sending missions to train leaders in co-operatives, with UNICEF in providing experts to run milk processing and pasteurizing plants. Again, in Iraq to deal with the flood emergency in 1954, FAO advisers co-operated in a common aid programme with experts from the United Nations Department of Social Affairs, from UNICEF and from the United Nations Relief and Works Agency (UNRWA). In 1952 an FAO mission went to Korea to collaborate with other United Nations experts in reconstruction problems. Co-operation between the United Nations agencies both in technical assistance and in the regular programme is becoming an increasingly prominent feature.

FAO programmes are able in some instances to complement the so-called " bilateral programmes " run by the more advanced countries. For instance, the United States International Co-operation Administration (ICA) is financing a large-scale irrigation programme in Iran, paying for the equipment and the public works expenditure involved, while FAO contributes water-use and crop experts to advise on how the irrigation water can be employed to best advantage. Pakistan asked FAO for expert irrigation advisers and, after they had devised a programme, Pakistan was able to obtain ICA finance from the United States to the extent of one million dollars. Ceylon had obtained through the Colombo Plan a great quantity of agricultural machinery to clear and cultivate huge areas in the Gal Oya valley, but she lacked mechanics to keep the machines running; so through FAO she obtained an expert who trained mechanics and fitters and set up workshops until when he left he could be confident the machinery would be regularly and adequately serviced. Therefore, although superficially the international picture appears confused in respect to technical aid with so many agencies operating simultaneously, in fact they keep in constant contact and find frequent opportunities for supplementing each others' activities.

Looking back now from 1955 over five years of ETAP and rather more than five years of technical assistance under FAO's regular programme, how would one measure the results? Altogether some 26.5 million dollars up to now have been spent by FAO alone in direct technical assistance to under-developed countries. Has this been worthwhile? What are the dividends?

Norris E. Dodd raised this same question shortly before he left FAO when he wrote:[1]

> It is always easier to describe the work in hand than to measure the results achieved. In many cases this report does

---

[1] *The Work of FAO, 1952/53.*

assess some advances, as for instance in the increased production of maize in Europe through the use of hybrid varieties, the rapid extension of fish culture in the Caribbean, in the Near East and Asia, exchanges of seed which will increase yields, the reduction of losses by the provision of grain storage facilities, the modernization of slaughter-houses and the construction of refrigerated warehouses.

The objectives..... of the Conference will be more effectively achieved by examples of progress made in particular countries than by the adoption of further resolutions and recourse to additional exhortation. The farmer who sees richer and better grain in his neighbour's fields, healthier and more productive livestock in his neighbour's farmyards, is more stimulated to improve his own practices by such examples than by debates, discussions, reports, pamphlets, or other printed matter. Similarly one country, realizing the benefit of the technical assistance which its neighbours are enjoying, will itself be the readier to prepare its own forward programme and request the help and advice which FAO stands ready to provide for converting those programmes into realization.

Of the many kinds of seed which FAO assistance has sown, only a few are quick to germinate; the majority by their nature will take some time to show results. The real harvest lies ahead. Thus the value of the work to date should be assessed not mainly on the basis of results already visible to the naked eye but on what is being prepared for the future. It would seem probable that the cumulative effects of what is being done through this programme will ultimately surpass the prophecies of the most extreme optimists.

FAO attempts to maintain a reasonable balance between programmes that have short-term immediate effects and longer-term ones in so far, that is, as it is in a position, through its mission chiefs and visits of its staff, to influence the requests of governments. Some programmes, such as locust control, plant protection, grain storage, forest fire protection, show quick, tangible results; others, such as the building of an extension service, ocean fisheries exploration, home nutrition instruction, show fruit much later.

The overall programme must have regard to other balances — between countries, not an undue share to any one; between technical fields, nutrition, forestry, fisheries, economics and statistics, agricultural production; between the scientific/technical on the one hand and the economic/social on the other. And it may be remarked that experience shows it much easier to impart expert advice in the former than in the latter field. The control of rinderpest with vaccines presents broadly the same problem in Ethiopia and Thailand but the attempt to establish agricultural credit co-operatives would be radically different in the one country from the other. It is clearly going to be more difficult to provide efficacious advice in fields which involve the *mores* of a people, since in these an expert is one who thoroughly understands the material with which he has to deal, which means someone steeped in the customs and traditions of the country being advised; and such experts are not readily found.

The quantity of technical assistance that can be usefully purveyed through international agencies depends at any one moment largely upon the amount of effort that the requesting country is able to exert, in terms of men and money, to help itself. The external aid should be only a pump-primer, not the bulk of the programme. Striking examples of large new government expenditures in connection with comparatively small technical assistance expenditures are found in Ceylon, India, Iraq and Brazil, to mention but a few. Some governments have already allocated public funds on a generous scale to agricultural development and are limited in granting more by the difficulty of raising further taxes from a population having a low level of income. Other governments, however, could, within the limits of funds now available to them, allocate more to food and agriculture with benefit to the whole economy. ETAP has to be geared to what governments are able and prepared to do themselves; beyond a point the law of diminishing returns will begin to operate.

Improvements in the administration of the programme are being made all the time. For one thing, governments are formulating better requests than in the early days. They have taken stock of their needs and resources, human and administrative; they have in many cases FAO mission chiefs whom they can consult; they can acquaint themselves with the types of aid available and can discuss how to adjust it to their needs.

The FAO Secretariat for its part has acquired knowledge and experience. It is now more skilled in selecting experts for jobs better chosen and defined. Its staff have assembled more intimate knowledge of the country situations and can therefore brief the designated expert far more throughly. It has learned what are the essential facilities in the country to enable the expert to perform his task. It has found out that the job does not end with the termination of the expert's assignment but, as was seen in the practical example above, includes a following-up service which helps to ensure that sufficient nationals have been trained to carry on the work initiated, that permanent equipment is acquired and that the whole is under the supervision of an administration with appropriate funds.

The method of financing the Technical Assistance Programme has certainly not helped its development. Whereas the ordinary budgets of specialized agencies such as FAO are regularly and automatically contributed in amounts based on decisions of the FAO biennial Conference the Technical Assistance Fund has been based on a voluntary pledge announced annually for the next succeeding year only by participating governments at the pledging conference. The organizations therefore have never known from one year to the next exactly what funds they would have available for technical assistance. More serious still is the fact that FAO must plan its programme for the following year in July and August, well before the pledging conference, and must put it in operation on 1 January, on which date it is by no means certain when the promised funds will have been paid in. This annual vote has not only complicated operations but naturally leaves experts in uncertainty as to the duration of their contracts. One year is usually too short a time for an expert to do more than find out what he has to do and take the first steps towards doing it. A second and often a third year are necessary, but FAO and the other agencies had to enter into commitments with a large number of experts with no guarantee that they would have the necessary funds to honour them.

The Technical Assistance Programme was, of course, an entirely new venture in international relationships, and from the beginning of its operation much was learned about the methods and techniques of giving technical assistance. Administrative problems relating to recruitment, utilization of currencies, supply of equipment, transport of experts and Fellows, all arose in early years and were dealt with. However, the conditions under which the programme is operated by the central intergovernmental body, the Technical Assistance Committee, and its Secretariat the Technical Assistance Board, have been subjected to constantly changing decisions. It is no exaggeration to say that the participating organizations have been thrown into an annual confusion and reorganization by considerable changes in policy which have rightly been described as " pulling up the plant to see how the roots are developing." There is no doubt that governments have a definite interest and responsibility in seeing that funds are most efficiently expended, but it will be for the good of the programme if it is now allowed to develop for a few years within the framework of policies which have been worked out on the basis of the first five years' experience.

Viewed from the angle of what the developed countries are prepared to do to aid the under-developed, ETAP must be counted a proud achievement; but viewed in the perspective of what has to be done by the under-developed countries themselves if they are to advance a measurable distance along the road to prosperity, the volume of effort appears puny indeed. Consider for example the amount of public expenditure on technical services for agriculture. The United States, taking Federal and State governments together, spends 535 dollars per annum per head of its agricultural population. A typical under-developed country spends on the same service 11 dollars per annum per head of population in agriculture. But it will be hard for the under-developed country to spend more until it can raise more taxes, and to raise more taxes it must first expand national income, which in turn requires revolutionary developments not only in agriculture and forestry but in industry and transport too. In the last analysis, it is true, the under-developed countries must help themselves; but, at present, operation bootstrap operates on a shoestring.

While this chapter has been mainly about agriculture (including nutrition, forestry and fisheries) it must not be forgotten that the technical assistance movement embraces other equally important aspects of human life. The United Nations has itself a technical assistance programme concerned with social welfare, public administration, roads, housing, and other fields. The World Health Organization has helped its Member Governments to establish effective health services and eradicate diseases such as malaria and yaws, which formerly afflicted millions of human beings; modern public health methods are in fact having a dramatic effect on vital statistics and population growth and hence on the relation between food supplies and requirements. Among the aims of UNESCO is the expansion of primary and secondary education throughout the world, and UNESCO legitimately claims that without education most other kinds of development are impossible. The ILO, founded at the same time as the League of Nations, seeks to improve working conditions and relations between employed and employers. UNICEF, well endowed because the welfare of children has a strong emotional appeal, finances large programmes for improving child health and nutrition, with technical co-operation from WHO and FAO.

Then there is "bilateral" aid, already referred to, that is, direct technical help rendered by prosperous technically advanced countries to others with still under-developed resources; help which, in the financial sense, has been on a scale beyond anything the United Nations and the specialized agencies have been able to provide. The United States is by far the most generous purveyor of "bilateral" aid, but other technically advanced countries, e.g. Canada, the United Kingdom, Australia and New Zealand have made substantial contributions, for example through the Colombo Plan.

Much of what has been said in this book with reference to FAO applies to the whole broad technical assistance field. The other organizations, international and national, which provide technical assistance have approximately similar difficulties to face and are animated by similar motives. But to say this is not to belittle the part which FAO has played and is playing in the undertaking. In its history, through Geneva, Hot Springs and Quebec, and the first ten years of its working life, FAO has never been far from the centre of the movement. It was in "food and agriculture" that many of the concepts and motives which underlie technical assistance first took shape.

In spite of all its technical and financial limitations, the Technical Assistance Programme must be reckoned worthwhile. It is something novel in the intercourse of nations. It constitutes a new essay by them in the ethic of equalizing opportunities; for the first time they are seeking to practise internationally what in varying degrees they already practise at home.

Of course there are frustrating aspects: the inadequate sums of money, the insecurity of having to rely on an annual vote in the legislatures of the contributing countries, the lack of an agency to purvey advice on industry, the unwillingness of some countries to make experts available for service. Yet surely what is remarkable is that the programme exists at all. In its first five years of life it has become immensely popular. Though many will make suggestions for adjustment and modification, no one wants to abandon it. "We are upon an engagement very difficult but the campaign must go on."

Chapter VIII

SPRINGBOARD FOR ACTION

Has anyone ever added up the amounts that the governments of the world spend each year directly upon food and agriculture? It must be an impressive figure, even though in the under-developed countries it falls far short of the desirable. In addition, they spend roughly 5.5 million dollars on the regular services of FAO (the annual contribution of the United States represents the price of one cigarette per American citizen) and another 5 to 7 million dollars on FAO's ETAP. By comparison with the first, as yet uncalculated figure, these contributions to the international activity are not burdensome.

Nevertheless, taxpayers view with more jaundiced eye that part of their taxes which goes into a pool to help "foreign" countries, so it is fair to ask what they have got, severally and collectively, in return for the, say 70 million dollars which they have spent on FAO (both programmes together), since the organization was born. What assets are there to report on to stockholders? What does the balance-sheet look like?

The first answer to this question is that investing in FAO means investment in a *growth* stock, one which should not be expected to develop fully its inherent value for a long time. Some small dividends are already being distributed but it would be unrealistic to expect sensational returns in the early years. Governments have already obtained for themselves through FAO an eminently satisfactory intelligence service, a lot of spade-work in international economic problems and an efficiently administered Technical Assistance Programme. They have sought through FAO to create for themselves a better environment in which to work for the Hot Springs objectives: better nutrition, more efficient production and distribution in agriculture, forestry and fisheries and improvement of rural welfare. The next decade will reap the fruit of this last decade's work.

We do not judge the result of the farmer's work ten days after he has sown his seed, nor that of FAO ten years after its birth. Maybe we judge the farmer at harvest after 100 days, with an eye open to see that his technique of husbandry will yield him as good or better harvests in succeeding years; maybe we judge FAO after the first 20 years and with a similar proviso.

Furthermore, whether the effort to work through FAO has been worthwhile will depend less upon the deeds of the past decade than upon what governments do in the next decade. If in the years ahead they pursue policies, nationally and internationally, which, although limited by the resources at their disposal and the support accorded by their articulate public opinion, consistently seek the objectives accepted at Hot Springs, then they should derive notable benefits from the FAO machinery. In most countries, developed and under-developed alike, the programmes in the FAO fields which governments have now in hand constitute an extraordinary advance on those of 1939 or even 1945; as to the further development of these programmes during the coming years, some lessons may be learned from the past and certain considerations borne in mind for the future.

First of all, in regard to production schemes as distinct from government services for agriculture, there appears to exist widely an emotional attraction to size for its own sake. The bigger the project, the better — almost unreservedly. Jungle clearance is planned in units of a million acres, irrigation through canals delivering 1,000 cusecs, settlement schemes by the thousand families. Many people cherish the fond belief, derived partly from the military, that the deployment of sufficient men and material will overcome any problem in nature; "the engineer can fix it" expresses their view. This mentality has been responsible for a tragic waste of money in recent years and there are signs that, particularly in certain underdeveloped countries, the wastage is still going on. But it is precisely the poorest countries that can least afford to make large costly mistakes. The more material and financial resources are limited, the more desirable is it to test and prove a large-scale proposal before becoming committed to it. Once the concrete has been poured and the distribution channels dug, it is too late to realize that the dam will silt up within two years or that there is no market for the particular crop which the newly irrigated land will produce.

It is recognized that governments are in a hurry; they are under public pressure to produce more food quickly, to get spectacular results. Unfortunately, there are few places where so much is already known of the environmental factors, physical, economic and social, governing the outcome of a scheme, that there need be no hesitation before embarking at full scale. Equally, unfortunately, there are too few instances of governments proceeding step by step: investigation, research, trials, pilot scheme, recruitment of managerial know-how and finally, if necessary and proved, the big project.

Greater expenditure on research is one of the most outstanding needs of the next ten years, in the underdeveloped countries themselves. Most of these lie between the tropics, whereas the bulk of agricultural research during the past 100 years has taken place and continues to be undertaken in the temperate zones. All too little is known about the behaviour of soils after bush clearance, varieties of crops adapted to tropical environments, responses to fertilizers under tropical and subtropical conditions, the control of the pests and diseases afflicting plants and livestock in these areas, the most suitable types of farm implements and machinery, and the true costs of mechanized as against manual farming. Those who are trying to farm in these areas of the world and who are eager for technical guidance in their operations, turn to the local government experiment station, if there is one, and find almost invariably that answers do not yet exist. It is common to deplore the "gap" which obtains in advanced countries between the level of scientific knowledge and farming practice. There is much to be said for the view that in the tropical and subtropical world the gap is even greater, for so little systematic knowledge has been accumulated that there is hardly any information to transmit to the more intelligent farmer.

During the past decade many governments have understandably given preference to projects yielding immediate fruit. They may now wish to consider the advisability of devoting more expenditure to research and field experimental work.

Beyond research the next stage will be experiment on a field scale leading into some kind of pilot scheme. It may be almost as disastrous to jump straight from the experiment station to the large scheme as to plunge into the large scheme without any research data at all. Pilot schemes enable valuable lessons to be learned before large funds are committed. You may, for instance, have established cocoa as a successful crop on your experiment station; but, if you then proceed to plant up 500 or 1,000 acres either for peasant family cultivation or as a plantation, you may find that squirrels eat the lot. This could have been ascertained on 50 acres with much less expenditure of money and without disappointing and perhaps antagonizing the settlers. Especially where the human factor is likely to play a decisive part in the success of a project, notably in settlement schemes, progress by stages has been found the most prudent course. If, for instance, the plan is to take some thousands of families out of their familiar environment and settle them in new surroundings where the whole ecology is different and where, further, they are being asked to grow unfamiliar crops by unfamiliar methods, then it is highly desirable to try with half-a-dozen families first and through them learn the problems, economic and social, perhaps anthropological, that may have to be solved. Thus, governments should consider the desirability of providing for the pilot scheme as a stage in the preparation of any large project and may wish to obtain, through FAO, expert advice on the layout of such schemes.

Since in most under-developed countries governments have to make a choice, often a hard one, between various schemes put forward as feasible and desirable, it is important to choose those that will stand the best chance of economic success. Governments can ill afford the odium of establishing a new farm community which finds it impossible to make a living or a production scheme that, instead of supporting itself, has to be subsidized out of public funds almost indefinitely. At present there is some evidence that insufficient attention is paid in advance to the economic viability of the development programmes. It is not enough to draw up a report in an office demonstrating in figures that an investment of, say, one million dollars on a project will produce a net revenue of 150,000 dollars per annum after providing for the incomes of the workers and all other expenses. Every element entering into that calculation requires to be tested and wherever possible put to practical proof before it is accepted as valid. Can that particular land be cleared for the sum mentioned? Has anyone tried and costed a few acres? Can the buildings be erected for that price? Are there any examples? What will the equipment and machinery cost to operate and service and has adequate allowance been made for depreciation and for the cost of holding spares? On what experience are the assumptions as to crop yields based? Have weed control, crop spraying and other protective measures been allowed for? Where will the product be marketed — locally or abroad — and what degree of certainty exists as to continuity of demand? What might the price be, say, five or ten years ahead, especially in the case of slow-maturing tree crops? Can men be recruited with adequate previous experience of the production, processing and marketing sides of the project? What incentives will there be for them as managers to make most economic and effective use of the funds put at their disposal? Have staff been provided to do the necessary minimum of costing and accounting? What else needs to be added perhaps in the way of transportation and public services (hospital, schools, etc.) to help the project succeed?

This illustrative, but by no means exhaustive, list of bread-and-butter questions does not exaggerate the number of matters that warrant investigation while a production project is being planned. It is a field in which expert advice might be as useful as in any scientific field. Just as in recent years the new profession of "chemical engineer" has come into existence, so what seems to be wanted here is an "economic engineer" to design, prepare specifications and draw out bills of quantities for the job. A more widespread adoption of this approach could contribute powerfully to avoidance of major disappointments.

Governments are paying increasing attention to the more general facilities which the farm population uses and which contribute to its prosperity; for example, farm credit facilities, crop financing and crop insurance; marketing facilities including slaughter-houses, refrigerated warehouses and railroad wagons, equipment for bulk handling of grain; and the services of experts in these matters will be in increasing demand. Statistical services, too, need strengthening in many under-developed countries both in respect of agricultural production and trade statistics and in the new field of consumption statistics and forecasting.

One of the main gaps in our knowledge of economic trends in these countries and even in some more developed ones relates to consumption. It has often been assumed that, in a country with a low average level of diet, food production could be expanded for a long time without creating any marketing difficulties, and those who took this view are surprised to find surpluses developing, not merely in export crops, but in staple foods for the domestic market while malnourishment and even undernourishment still prevails. They tended to ignore the truism that the supply in the domestic market has to be matched against the purchasing power of the non-farm population. If the supply expands faster than this purchasing power, prices will fall and/or surpluses accumulate. Leaving aside the case of bumper harvests which should be dealt with by storage policies, there may already be instances of agricultural improvement out-distancing the success being achieved in raising the purchasing power of other sections of the population. It should be possible now to predict this purchasing power (techniques of national income estimating are being applied to under-developed countries) and the types and quantities of food which the various income-groups may be expected to purchase. Related to the general development tempo of the country, this would give some idea for a year or two ahead of what quantities of each of the principal categories of food would be likely to be absorbed at given prices. Armed with these forecasts, governments would be better placed for influencing by price policy or otherwise the re-orientation and adjustment of crop and livestock, forestry and fishery programmes. This is one of the ideas which FAO experts try to develop in regional meetings.

To increase national prosperity workers must work more productively and to do this they must enjoy not merely better education but also better health and nutrition. Many governments which formerly spent considerable sums on health have, during this last decade, begun to spend modestly on nutrition too; on school feeding schemes, on nutrition education, on training nutrition workers, on nutrition surveys. As the value of this work becomes increasingly apparent, FAO may expect increased calls for aid in this field; already the last session of the Conference voted an increase in the budget of the Nutrition programme.

During the last few years nutrition research workers have discovered that malnutrition due to lack of protein is common in most under-developed countries, a discovery which has important repercussions on food production policy since it accentuates the need for a larger production of animal and vegetable foods rich in protein. The marriage between health and agriculture, celebrated 20 years ago, remains a stable partnership ready to assume new obligations as scientific knowledge grows.

A similar trend is apparent in respect of agricultural extension or advisory services; more governments becoming convinced that funds must somehow be allocated to creating or expanding this service. Most are still at the stage where training of staff — leaders at all levels — is the prerequisite, and it is for training that the majority of requests for experts will be received. In extension work an important contribution can and is often made by farm organizations in countries where they are well established. At present, farm organizations are strongest in industrial countries such as the United States, Japan and the United Kingdom; in less developed countries if they exist it is often to defend a particular crop or social class. It might well be that by encouraging the formation of democratic, general-purpose farm organizations in under-developed countries, government could get a substantial amount of extension work done more cheaply, and anyway with less drain on public funds, than under its own auspices.

Agrarian reform is another programme of which more will be heard in the coming decade. This embraces reforms of tenure legislation, land redistribution, prevention of fragmentation and consolidation of holdings. The programme aims at providing greater equality of opportunity to those working on the land, enabling those who prove to have real farming ability to get land and use it. It should seek to balance security of tenure with flexibility, to provide incentives and opportunities to agricultural investment, to improve the size and layout of holdings. It is a field notoriously difficult for experts to advise in, since it involves appreciation of the entire social structure of the country, the traditions and habits of its people. As indicated earlier, foreigners have to live a long time in the country before they have the highest competence to aid in this type of programme. Nonetheless, since governments will undoubtedly seek outside help, special care must be taken in recruiting advisers.

Millions of food producers throughout the world still use time-honoured agricultural methods, to which the life of the community is adjusted. The introduction of modern technology, in agriculture as in other fields, necessarily raises a host of social problems, and awareness of these is essential if technical assistance is to be successful. Hence increasing emphasis should be placed on the study of community life and ways and means of influencing ordinary men and women, particularly women, so that they may derive full benefits from the gifts which technology can offer. The development of agricultural extension, home economics and social services can facilitate this all-important adjustment. It is significant that the Economic and Social Council is becoming more and more concerned with the social aspects of human progress. Significantly also its debates show that many problems in the social field are still undefined and the action needed to solve them equally undetermined.

Governments, particularly of the smaller under-developed countries, are showing increasing interest in co-operating with neighbouring small countries in regional programmes. Hitherto these have been either training centres or some pest or disease control programme (locusts, foot-and-mouth), and there will unquestionably be more such. But, having observed the usefulness of combined activity, governments may well wish to apply it in other spheres. For instance, certain lines of research (and as much in fisheries and forestry as in agriculture) suggest themselves as suitable for a regional experiment station jointly sponsored by a group of governments and with expert supervision obtained through FAO.

Another regional activity coming into greater demand is the joint meeting between governments for the purpose of programme review and outlook discussion. In this the developed show as much desire to co-operate as the under-developed countries; they have as many problems of adjustment; perhaps more, to the extent that they depend more on external markets and less on self-sufficiency. Much might be done over the next years to make these meetings more effective; documentation should be improved when more countries have developed their statistical services; readiness to disclose plans could be more marked, willingness to discuss adjustments more widespread among delegations. But these meetings, whatever their present drawbacks, do provide a forum more intimate and less unwieldy than the full Conference, in which government representatives can for a moment step outside their national preoccupations and deliberate upon the foreign repercussions of their domestic agricultural policies.

At the world level, governments have the responsibility through FAO of making ETAP work effectively in the field of food and agriculture. Some of them already appreciate the grievous effects of the annual budget vote procedure in preventing their obtaining from FAO other than quite short-term assignments of experts and preventing FAO from planning an economical utilization of its own staff. As more governments come to this view, it may be hoped that the procedures for providing finance will be modified so as to provide longer-term assurances. Also, some of the restrictions imposed upon the administration of ETAP funds do more to hamper the work than to ensure honest accounting. Reforms of administrative procedures make an undistinguished debate but they may decisively influence the efficiency of the programmes.

There is one international subject-field in which it is difficult to foresee what governments will want to do together and what services they will ask of FAO: the field of commodity policy, price stabilization and surplus disposal schemes. As appeared in Chapter V, governments have been wary of undertaking international commitments over the last few years, and there is no reason to suppose that this sentiment will change, short of a general economic crisis or special trouble in regard to individual commodities. This attitude, as has been seen, rests logically upon governments' intense preoccupation with defending agricultural prosperity in their own countries and their desire to keep their hands free to initiate any national measures necessary for this purpose. It will prove far harder to co-ordinate 70 government-regulated agricultures than 70 laissez-faire ones. There are grounds, therefore, for expecting only slow progress in this field during the coming decade. Governments will be willing to co-operate with the Secretariat in further methodological discussions and from time to time to frame and secure acceptance of statements of general principles with reference to some special part of the field. One useful lesson has already been learnt, that this type of international discussion is generally better undertaken by people closely in touch with government thinking. The expertise acquired by the Secretariat in its continuing servicing of committees and working parties is already and will increasingly become a positive factor for progress.

It seems, on the other hand, more likely that governments will make progress in setting up machinery for international financing of development, such as the International Finance Corporation and the proposed SUNFED. Though consideration of these lies outside the immediate purview of an account of FAO, the progress that can be made in increasing the amount of financial aid for well-conceived development projects will powerfully contribute to the creation of an economic environment in which agriculture, forestry and fisheries can be modernized.

The future of FAO depends basically upon what governments are prepared to do in their own countries and, consequently, with each other through the organization they created for that purpose. That is why most of this chapter has been occupied with discussion of the activities which governments themselves are likely to develop in food and agriculture during the coming decade, rather than future activities of the Secretariat. The more they do, the more FAO will be needed. To say this is not to deny the role of the Director-General and his Secretariat in suggesting, advising, stimulating, sometimes leading. Indeed a corps of international civil servants occupies a somewhat novel position not entirely analogous to that of a national civil service. Because they are responsible to scores of different sovereign national authorities constantly changing in their personnel and opinions, only intermittently producing any corporate pronouncements, the Secretariats of the United Nations and the specialized agencies, of necessity, take an increased responsibility for evolving what come to be adopted as intergovernmental policies. A secretariat which has established a reputation for efficient and courteous service will command respect and may, on occasion, fashion courses of action on which governments find themselves able to agree.

Finally, there is one respect in which governments can strengthen the work of FAO, and that is by having themselves effectively represented at meetings of committees, Council and Conference. Nothing indicates more clearly lack of interest in and appreciation of this intergovernmental endeavour than the sending of second-class officials to represent governments at conferences. Immediately after the war the standard of representation was uniformly high. Governments must not rely overmuch on the Secretariat. The work is work by governments for governments, and its quality will depend on the quality of the men sent by governments to carry it out. For expert meetings experts, not diplomats, are in order; for the FAO Council, the administrative head of at least one government department and, on occasion of special debates, even a minister; for the Conference, always a minister (and preferably the minister for agriculture) plus one or two department heads and appropriate advisers. Now that the Conference of FAO meets only every other year, this should not be too much to ask.

CHAPTER IX

THE MARCH OF EVENTS

The application of science to the amelioration of man's material condition has been going on for centuries, at an accelerating tempo. The assumption by governments of responsibility for the economic prosperity, in addition to the political security, of their respective countries is a phenomenon of the last 30 to 40 years. The attempt to effect some integration at the international level of national economic policies is a creature of the last ten years. It is these three factors — the continuing scientific revolution, the growth of governmental direction and the need for international co-ordination — which, applied to food and agriculture, have brought FAO into existence and have shaped its growth in the formative years.

Whither are these forces pushing nations in regard to food and agriculture? What will be the effect on the uses to which they wish to put FAO? What changes in the structure of world society may come to pass?

As to science, every evidence suggests that the law of accelerating motion applies to the number and significance of its discoveries. We ought to anticipate that the inventions of the coming decade will make those of the past decade look small by comparison. We cannot foresee in what fields the next advances will occur, but we can be sure that the world's scientific workers are always upon the threshold of something dramatic and exciting, something of deep significance to the material and spiritual well-being of mankind.

Often indeed the scientific and technological innovations catch us unawares and we fail, for a time at least, to adjust our social behaviour and our ethical principles. There have been many instances in what are now the advanced countries, but just now some peril lies in countries which are suddenly acquiring the tools of modern life before their people have adjusted their *mores,* and acquired the habits of obedience to law and of political tolerance. If among a few of the persons new to government, one sometimes observes tough dealings, unscrupulous behaviour and moral weakness, it is well to remember that similar behaviours characterized the social and political life of the now advanced countries less than two centuries ago.

As to the role of governments, it is the continuing scientific revolution itself, coupled with the ethical urge to more equal opportunity, which oblige governments to extend the scope of their intervention and to set up more administrative machinery. It seems the only way to keep the environment under control. We may be reasonably confident that in the coming years the responsibilities placed by the public on governments for ensuring prosperity and securing fair shares will be increased rather than diminished. And if the governments do not produce results they will be thrown out. This popular clamour creates difficulties enough in the advanced countries in which governments are fortunate in having at their disposal staffs of trained, loyal servants, a large mass of relevant information and traditions of stable institutions; it creates almost insuperable problems in under-developed countries where these advantages are absent or still in embryo. Yet it is in these countries that governments assume the biggest burden, taking many of the largest industrial developments under their wing instead of leaving them to private enterprise. In these circumstances it is small wonder that they experience difficulty in raising funds and in finding the cadres to promote simultaneously the scientific revolution in agriculture. But these very difficulties impel those governments to look more abroad for technical and financial aid, and generally speaking they prefer to obtain aid through international agencies than from a single advanced country, not only because the former will be free from any suspicion of "imperialism" but also because they have access to a wider range of skills and can offer a greater choice of external training facilities.

Up till now the amount of aid that the advanced countries are prepared to channel through international agencies represents a comparatively small part of the total; in the main they keep assistance under their individual direct control. There is reason to expect, as well as hope, that the balance will gradually shift in favour of international administration, but it must take time. The sentiment of kinship with far-off peoples is weak, the impulse to collaborate is new. At the national level the public conscience demands a large measure of economic fair shares, of income redistribution, and calls upon its governments to effect it; so, gradually, at the international level public opinion will become increasingly redistribution-minded and will require its governments to act through international agencies. The trend is plain; though it may have temporary setbacks, the impulse toward treating your neighbour as yourself (and including the most distant peoples as neighbours) cannot be denied.

Meanwhile, the advanced countries will continue doing (some of) the right things for (some of) the wrong reasons. The "western powers," as propaganda for democratic capitalism, will put large resources at the disposal of the more "uncommitted" of the under-developed countries, and indeed the "eastern powers" may compete in the same areas at the same game. The United States Government, under pressures, may switch from aid to loan type of assistance in her bilateral programmes. The metropolitan powers may vote larger sums for welfare in their colonial territories to stave off independence movements. There are many who support assisting the under-developed countries and territories chiefly on the ground that it provides wider export markets for the advanced countries and helps them to maintain full employment at home.

It is not cynical to welcome and use all these motives in combination for a right cause. It is more difficult to mobilize them for joint action in the commercial sphere of international relations, in trade and commodity policy. Here no ethical motive of "do-good-ism" comes into play, only self-interest; and, exceptions apart, governments are not persuaded that agreements to co-ordinate trade and commodity policy are in their best self-interest. Even quite severe fluctuations in prices such as were experienced in connection with the Korean war, seem to them a lesser evil than being tied to commitments which might hinder them from taking needed remedial measures in face of some domestic economic crisis. Only a major depression on a world-wide scale would quickly modify government sentiments on this question. But such a depression might have an opposite effect on the other wing of international activity; it might make governments feel obliged to cut back their contributions to international aid. It is therefore difficult to visualize forces in the coming decade which would stimulate advances on both fronts at once. The Secretariat, sitting at its vantage point, can see the logic and the reason for taking steps toward closer international collaboration, but it is the legislators, the ministers and their officials who have to be persuaded.

So far we have spoken of the trends which may be discerned with some degree of certainty. But in the web of human affairs there are more obscure threads, less subject to conscious control, much less predictable, which nevertheless may largely determine the destiny of us all. If this survey is to give a fairly balanced picture of what may lie ahead, it is right to end by referring to some of these "open issues."

One, which has figured much in the preceding discussion, is the tense race between population and production. While it would be rash indeed to predict the outcome, one cannot but feel that the production runner has stamina for many a spurt in the laps ahead. There are plant breeders working quietly somewhere today producing varieties which, through vigour and disease resistance, may revolutionize yields 10-20 years hence; similar advances may emerge from current work with livestock. Perhaps by then we shall find ourselves able to produce more food than is wanted; if so, we ought to be able to provide other occupations for the redundant labour. If, on the other hand, food output began to lag seriously, a general rise in prices of food as compared with other goods could not be resisted and nations would have to divert additional effort and resources to agriculture. We cannot say which way the cards will fall, but we can be equipped to deal with either contingency.

What of the low-income countries? Are we in the coming decade and thereafter working toward a position in which they will have living standards such as the richer countries have today? Are there not fewer unused resources compared with those upon which Europe could draw during her great spurt in the nineteenth century? Indubitably there are no new prairies, only difficult savannahs and rain forests — unless we learn to wrest food from the semi-frozen zones, the deserts and the oceans. But what we call a "resource" is nothing more than a piece of nature that man, because he has an appropriate technique, can exploit for his benefit. Learn a new technique and something hitherto valueless suddenly becomes a "resource" — witness uranium. Who can tell what new tools we shall devise or stumble upon.

And what of one particular resource — power — without which all else comes to a standstill? Coal is apparently giving out; some predict that oil will be used up; hydro-electric possibilities certainly seem limited. But now there is the promise of atomic energy in industrial use and the strong hope that in the fairly near future it will provide cheaper power than ever before. If so, it should have profound consequences. It will be the most easily transportable of all forms of power; atomic plants could be erected almost anywhere. Thus jobs could be taken to the people instead of the people to the jobs, reducing the headaches of international migration. And no special industrial advantages to countries possessing coal or oil. We cannot yet discern what this new gift has in store for us.

Then there is the vital economic problem of capital formation in the under-developed countries. How can savings be accumulated from people with extremely low incomes on a scale sufficient to build a modern industrial community? Mathematically it can be demonstrated impossible. Politically (and socially) the attempt must occasion tremendous tensions. It involves the discipline of compelling the people to forego present consumption in order that capital goods may be created and industry expanded. In the absence of such a discipline, there may be revolutions and counter-revolutions; there will doubtless be periodic inflation and balance-of-payments crises. Yet, as was pointed out in Chapter I, if we were living in, say, the year 1750 would it not appear equally hopeless for the poverty-stricken people of Europe ever to accumulate the capital which they then proceeded to acquire? Was not much of the wealth concentrated in the hands of "idle rich" who squandered it and was not its sum total derisory, even if it had been mobilized for production? We could scarcely have been more optimistic about Europe's chances then than we can be about the under-developed countries' chances now.

But are not the rich nations getting richer so fast that the gap between them and the poorer nations is widening? Yes, on the evidence that seems to be the case. However, it has happened before on the national level. One of the first consequences of the industrial revolution was to concentrate wealth more than before into few hands — large landowners and captains of industry; only much later did equalizing forces assert themselves and then not through the market but primarily through politics and the political instrument of fiscal legislation. Internationally the gap may well go on widening for a little while yet; but we have already noted examples of peoples and governments beginning to desire to apply the national doctrine of equal opportunity and fairer shares in the international sphere. One may predict confidently that this sentiment will grow, though it is not possible to say through what policies it will work towards its objectives.

These then are some of the open questions which tantalize us as we peer into the future. And there is one final question: what will the material and social and spiritual relationships between nations be like when the differences in standards of living between rich countries and poor countries are not greater than the income differences of the richest and the poorest classes within, say, Sweden or New Zealand today? We can be fairly sure that in such circumstances the nations will make extemely full use of international agencies; for, just as there is more international trade between two wealthy nations than between one rich and one poor one, so there will be more intercourse of all kinds and more co-operative co-ordination thereof. To the extent that the peoples strive — and it is in man's nature to strive — steadfastly towards these goals of developing the riches of the earth, opening wider opportunities to the under-privileged and securing fairer shares as between nations, we may be sure that an agency like FAO, with all it stands for and all the services it provides, will be wanted more and more.

APPENDIX I

LIST OF MEMBER NATIONS

Afghanistan
Argentina
Australia
Austria
Belgium
Bolivia
Brazil
Burma
Cambodia
Canada
Ceylon
Chile
Colombia
Costa Rica
Cuba
Denmark
Dominican Republic
Ecuador
Egypt
El Salvador
Ethiopia
Finland
France
Germany, Federal Republic
Greece
Guatemala
Haiti
Honduras
Iceland
India
Indonesia
Iran
Iraq
Ireland
Israel
Italy

Japan
Jordan
Korea
Laos
Lebanon
Liberia
Luxembourg
Mexico
Nepal
Netherlands
New Zealand
Nicaragua
Norway
Pakistan
Panama
Paraguay
Peru
Philippine Republic
Portugal
Saudi Arabia
Spain
Sweden
Switzerland
Syria
Thailand
Turkey
Union of South Africa
United Kingdom
United Kingdom of Libya
United States of America
Uruguay
Venezuela
Viet-Nam
Yemen
Yugoslavia

Appendix II

SELECTED LIST OF PUBLICATIONS

The preparation and distribution of publications constitute one of FAO's major services to its Member Governments. Publications are an indispensable means of giving effect to many aspects of the Organization's programme and their production is a central part of FAO's constitutional duties.

FAO's publications are directed mainly to administrators, technicians and other specialists, but they are also of interest to many other groups, persons and users in the broad field of human activity which the Organization's programme embraces.

The Organization's publications range from brief pamphlets to substantial reference works, and are issued as regular periodicals (monthly, bi-monthly, quarterly, or yearly); as technical studies within special numbered series; or as separate *ad hoc* monographs or reports. Prepared primarily by staff members, they also draw upon the knowledge and experience of consultants and specialists in many countries and in their sum total are the product of extensive, continuing co-operation between governments and experts the world over.

The principal publications are issued in English, French and Spanish editions and are available through the Organization's sales agents or distributors in a large number of countries.

The following provides a brief view of the more significant publications.

General

The principal documents in this category are the *Constitution, Rules and Regulations*; the Director-General's reports on *The Work of FAO* and *Activities of FAO under the Expanded Technical Assistance Programme*, which provide a general review of the work of the Organization year by year, under the regular programme and ETAP respectively; *The State of Food and Agriculture*; and the *Reports* of the various sessions of the Council and the Conference.

The State of Food and Agriculture, issued annually since 1947, reviews the world agricultural situation and presents outlook statements. Problems and trends of world-wide significance are analysed; production and trade figures are given in some detail region by region and commodity by commodity. In the 1955 edition the whole post-war decade was reviewed and the main issues ahead discussed.

STATISTICAL YEARBOOKS

The Organization publishes regularly three yearbooks, briefly described hereunder.

Yearbook of Food and Agricultural Statistics. This yearbook consists of two volumes: I. *Production;* II. *Trade.*

The *Production* volume is a reference book of basic statistics for all concerned with the study of agricultural development throughout the world. It covers annually the statistics on land use, crops, livestock numbers and products, food supplies and their utilization, means of production, prices and index numbers. The *Trade* volume gives the quantities of imports and exports of all major food and agricultural commodities, together with total estimates for regions and the world as a whole.

Yearbook of Forest Products Statistics. A section on the salient features of the world forest products situation is followed by production and trade statistics for roundwood, processed wood, wood pulp and pulp products. Other tables show the world trade in forest products.

Yearbook of Fishery Statistics. This yearbook consists of two volumes: I. *Production and Craft;* II. *International Trade.*

Production and Craft contains statistics of catch and landings, utilization (disposition), production of preserved and processed commodities, and fishing craft. *International Trade* presents figures on imports and exports of fishery products.

AGRICULTURE

The Agriculture Division comprises five branches concerned with Land and Water Use, Plant Production, Animal Production, Agricultural Institutions and Services, and Rural Welfare. Publications growing out of the programmes of these branches appear normally in either of two numbered series, the Agricultural Development Papers or Agricultural Studies series.

Development Papers, of which some 52 issues have appeared, are technical papers intended for use of leaders of agricultural development projects and include short monographs, reports of technical meetings, etc. Typical issues are: *Cereal Breeding Procedures, Equipment for the Processing of Tea, Problems of Animal Feeding in Europe, Small Farm Implements* and reports of the meetings of the Working Parties of the International Rice Commission on fertilizers and rice breeding.

The Agricultural Studies series, 28 of which have been issued to date, is composed of more substantial monographs on a somewhat higher technical or scientific level than the Development Papers, and include such studies as *Breeding Livestock Adapted to Unfavorable Environments, The Efficient Use of Fertilizers, Legumes in Agriculture, Improving the World's Grasslands, Milk Pasteurization;* studies on weed control, food refrigeration and Zebu cattle ; and certain reports issued jointly with the World Health Organization on brucellosis and zoonosis.

Among publications not included in these series may be mentioned a *Multilingual Vocabulary of Soil Science* (in eight languages), a *Bibliography on Land Tenure,* and an *Annotated Bibliography of Rice Soils and Fertilizers.*

The Agriculture Division also produces the *FAO Plant Protection Bulletin,* which makes available information received by the World Reporting Service on Plant Diseases and Pests. Issued monthly, it publishes reports on the occurrence, outbreak and control of pests and diseases of plants and plant products of economic significance and related topics.

Economics

The Economics Division comprises three branches concerned with Economic Analysis, Commodities, and Statistics.

In addition to the *Yearbook of Food and Agricultural Statistics,* mentioned above, the Economics Division issues the *Monthly Bulletin of Agricultural Economics and Statistics,* which to a large extent keeps the annual volumes up to date. Each issue also contains one or two articles on matters of current interest in the field of agricultural economics and an extensive section devoted to commodity notes.

Commodity problems and policies are dealt with in three numbered series.

The Commodity Policy Studies consist of analytical studies of international policies for agricultural products. Seven issues have appeared to date, including studies on the International Wheat Agreement, the International Sugar Agreement, the uses of agricultural surpluses to finance economic development in under-developed countries, and the stabilization of the international trade in rice.

Commodity Series bulletins are comprehensive studies reviewing production and trade developments in individual commodities: e.g., livestock and meat, fats and oils, fibres, grain, wheat, rice, sugar, fertilizers, cocoa, tobacco, tea, etc.

Commodity Reports provide brief appraisals of the current situation in individual commodities together with some indications of trends in the near future.

A major undertaking of FAO is the *Report on the 1950 World Census of Agriculture,* to be completed in three volumes which will together make up a comprehensive survey of the world's agricultural resources. It will provide basic information for planning what should be done, and where, to raise world production and to improve the agrarian structure. The first instalment of Volume I, *Census Results by Countries,* was published in March 1955, and includes the results of 32 countries and territories; the complete volume will contain the census results of about 100 countries.

FISHERIES

The Fisheries Division comprises three branches concerned with Fisheries Biology, Fisheries Technology, and Fisheries Economics.

In addition to the *Yearbook of Fishery Statistics,* mentioned above, the Division issues two periodicals; the *FAO Fisheries Bulletin* and *World Fisheries Abstracts.*

Published quarterly, the *FAO Fisheries Bulletin* presents analyses of recent fisheries developments, economic notes, statistical tables on landings and production of certain fisheries commodities, reports of fisheries activities of FAO, and notes on recent fisheries publications and films.

World Fisheries Abstracts is a bi-monthly review of technical literature on fisheries and related industries, covering the fields of fisheries technology, processing methods, boat design, fishing methods, chemical examination of fisheries products, etc.

Monographs in the Fisheries Studies series are *Salted Cod and Related Species*, *Commodity Standards for Fisheries Products*, and *Fish Farming and Inland Fishery Management in Rural Economy*.

Forestry

The Forestry Division comprises three branches devoted respectively to Forest Policy and Conservation, to Forest Research and Technology and to Forest Economics. Publications growing out of the programmes of these branches appear normally in either of two numbered series, Forestry Studies or Forestry Development Papers, or as separate unnumbered monographs.

Forestry Studies are substantial studies of major forestry questions. Typical issues are *Forest Policy, Law and Administration; Grazing and Forest Economy; National Forest Policies in Europe;* and *Research in Forestry and Forest Products*.

Forestry Development Papers are concerned with more specialized matters and are frequently preparatory to the production of a larger work. Thus, *Tree-Planting Practices for Arid Areas, Handling Forest Tree Seed, Tree Seed Notes* and other volumes may eventually be assembled in a revised form in a World Forest Planting Manual.

The separate unnumbered monographs include *World Forest Resources* (1955), which gives the results of the world-wide inventory undertaken by FAO in 1953. Others are *Paper for Printing*, issued jointly with UNESCO, and *European Timber Trends and Prospects*, published in collaboration with ECE.

The Division issues a quarterly publication, *Unasylva*, a review of forestry and forest products, containing articles on world conditions and developments; reports on world, regional and technical conferences; commodity reports on forest products; news items and reviews.

Nutrition

The Nutrition Division issues a series of Nutritional Studies which includes volumes on *Food Composition Tables for International Use, Dietary Surveys, School Feeding, Rice and Rice Diets, Teaching Better Nutrition, Calorie Requirements,* and occasional studies of local situations such as nutrition work in Greece, and of special problems such as Kwashiorkor in Africa and Central America.

An important recent publication is *Protein Malnutrition,* containing the proceedings of a Conference sponsored jointly by FAO, WHO, and the Josiah Macy Jr. Foundation.

Among the Division's unnumbered publications may be mentioned *Material on Home Economics and Its Teaching,* which assembles information on this subject drawn from many countries.

The Nutrition Meetings series contains reports of technical conferences and committees sponsored by FAO or by FAO jointly with the World Health Organization.

Legislation

FAO's Legislative Service issues a quarterly publication, *Food and Agricultural Legislation,* which contains a selection of food and agricultural laws and regulations of international importance. Texts of legislation are, according to their special interest, reproduced in full, in extract form or summarized.

Information Service

In addition to the usual press and radio communiques, the Information Service issues a few publications intended to inform the general public of the nature and progress of FAO's activities. *FAO Memo* is a monthly news bulletin issued gratis in regional editions in Europe (English and French), Latin America (Spanish), Near East (Arabic and English), Far East (Hindi and English), and North America (English). It is usually distributed in collaboration with National FAO Committees, some of which have national FAO news-letters. *FAO Picture Sheets* (English, French, Spanish) are a series used not only as educational posters in schools, etc., but to serve picture-using publications. These are distributed in limited quantities from Headquarters and Regional Offices. Other publications are *ad hoc* leaflets.

Appendix III

TRAINING CENTRES

Nutrition Training Course for nutrition workers from French-speaking territories south of the Sahara, held at Marseilles from April to July 1952, in collaboration with WHO.

Far Eastern Course on Economic Appraisal of Development Projects, held at Lahore, Pakistan, from October to December 1950, in co-operation with the Government of Pakistan, the International Bank and ECAFE.

Far Eastern Training Centre on Lumber Grading, held in Malaya for six weeks from 7 January 1952.

Far Eastern FAO/WHO Nutrition Training Course, held in Calcutta from September to December 1951, in co-operation with the Government of India.

Latin American Training Centre on Agricultural Census Tabulation Methods, held at Bogotá in January 1950.

Latin American Training Centre on Agricultural and Allied Plans and Projects, held in Chile, and sponsored by the Government of Chile, FAO, UN (including the Economic Commission for Latin America) and the International Bank, operated from 27 September to 21 December 1951.

Latin American Fisheries Training Centre, held at Valparaiso, from 6 January 1952 for ten weeks, in co-operation with the Government of Chile.

Latin American Training Centre for Agricultural Statistics, held at San José, Costa Rica, from 8 January 1951 for three months in co-operation with the Governments of Costa Rica and the USA, the Inter-American Statistical Institute, the Organization of American States, and UN.

East Mediterranean Training Centre in Economic Appraisal of Development Projects, held at Ankara, from 27 September to 21 December 1951, in collaboration with the International Bank and the Government of Turkey.

International Training Centre on Soil Fertility, Coimbatore, held for three months from July to October 1952.

International Training Centre on Rice Breeding, held at Cuttack from September to December 1952, in co-operation with the Government of India.

International Training Centre on Living Virus Vaccines, held at Izatnagar, Uttar Pradesh from 16 February to 7 March 1953, in co-operation with the Government of India.

Power Alcohol Seminar, held at Lucknow in October/November 1952, jointly sponsored by UNTAA, FAO, ECAFE and the Government of India.

Fish Culture Seminar, held at Djakarta during six weeks from May to June 1952, in co-operation with the Government of Indonesia.

Far Eastern Mechanical Logging Training Centre, held from 3 October 1952 to 23 March 1953, and based on the College of Forestry, Laguna, near Manila, for approximately two months of the period, while the remaining four months were spent in the field at centres based on four of the largest logging operations in the Philippines.

Rice Grading Training Centre, held in Thailand for eight weeks during March and April 1953, in co-operation with the Government of Thailand.

Indo-Pacific Fisheries Statistics Training Centre, held at Bangkok for six weeks during June and July 1952, in co-operation with the Government of Thailand.

Far Eastern Demonstration Centre for Agricultural Statistical Sampling, held at Bangkok for six months from September 1952 to March 1953, with the co-operation of the Government of Thailand.

FAO/ILO Near East Co-operatives Training Centre, held in Cyprus for three months from September to December 1952, with the co-operation of the Government of Cyprus.

Seminar in Experimental Design, held during July and August 1952 in Israel.

Seminar on Price and Production Statistics, held in Beirut from 1 to 14 July 1952, in co-operation with the Government of Lebanon, UNTAA, the Statistical Office of the United Nations.

The Near East Regional Agricultural Extension Development Centre, held at Beirut from 6 to 16 January 1953.

Seminar on Advanced Sampling, held at Stockholm in November 1952.

Eucalyptus Study Tour, held during September and October 1952, in co-operation with the Commonwealth of Australia.

Rural Electrification Study Group Meeting, held in Geneva for one month in October/November 1952.

Latin American Seminar on Land Problems, held at São Paolo for about five weeks during May and June 1953, in co-operation with the Brazilian Government, the UN Economic Commission for Latin America, the Organization of American States and the International Bank.

UN Rural Welfare Seminar, held at Rio de Janeiro for three weeks in January and February 1953, in co-operation with the Government of Brazil and several Brazilian organizations.

International Seminar on Statistical Organization, held in Ottawa from 13-31 October 1952, in co-operation with the Government of Canada, the UN Statistical Office, and other United Nations and international agencies.

International Study Course on Soil Conservation and Management, held in Chile from August to November 1952, in co-operation with the American Institute of Agricultural Science and the Government of Chile.

Latin American Fisheries Training Centre, held at Valparaiso, Chile from January to March 1952

Latin American Training and Demonstration Centre for Application of Agricultural Statistical Techniques, held in Ecuador for three-and-a-half months from July to October 1952, in co-operation with the Government of Ecuador and the UN Statistical Office.

Central American Credit Seminar, held in Guatemala during September and October 1952 jointly by FAO, the Economic Commission for Latin America (ECLA) and the Government of Guatemala.

Andean Agricultural Extension Training Centre, held in Peru for 12 weeks from 15 May to 8 August 1953, in co-operation with the Government of Peru and SCIPA (Servicio Cooperativo Interamericano de Producción de Alimentos).

Training Centre in Agricultural Statistics, held at Ibadan, Nigeria, with the co-operation of the Commission for Technical Co-operation in Africa south of the Sahara (CCTA), and the Government of Nigeria.

Dairy Training Centre, held in India towards the end of 1954.

Agricultural Extension Training Centre, held in Greece in late 1954.

Training Centre on Agricultural Extension Methods, held at Wageningen, the Netherlands in 1953, in co-operation with the Mutual Security Administration.

Co-operatives Training Centre (Caribbean Commission), held during 1954.

Fisheries Training School, held at Mexico from October to December 1954.

Training Centre on Agricultural Extension (Peru), held during 1953, with the collaboration of the Government of Peru and SCIPA.

Pasture and Range Management Course, held in the Argentine in collaboration with the Organization of American States and the Government of Argentina, in late 1953.

Training Centre on Production, Distribution and Utilization of Milk, held in Costa Rica with the co-operation of the Government of that country, during the second half of 1953.

Pulp and Paper Survey and Training Centre, held in Rio de Janeiro in September 1954, in collaboration with the Government of Argentina.

Training Centre on Range, Pasture and Fodder Development, held at Ankara, Turkey, from 5 June to 31 July 1954.

Animal Gynaecology Training Centre, held at Stockholm for ten months from 1 September 1954, in co-operation with the Governments of Sweden and India.

Mediterranean Agricultural Sampling and Demonstration Centre, held in Turkey from April to July 1955.

Training Centre in Statistical Sampling, held in Argentina for three months from June 1955.

FAO/US Training Course on Tropical Forestry, held at Puerto Rico in May 1955.